SMELLS LIKE BACON

the**skit**guys
GUIDE TO LIFELONG FRIENDSHIPS

EDDIE JAMES & TOMMY WOODARD
with Rene Gutteridge

K-LOVE BOOKS

K-LOVE Books
5700 West Oaks Blvd
Rocklin, CA 95765
Copyright © 2021

Printed in the United States of America.

First edition: 2021
10 9 8 7 6 5 4 3 2 1

ISBN: 978-1-954201-07-1 (hardcover)
ISBN: 978-1-954201-10-1 (trade paper)
ISBN: 978-1-954201-08-8 (eBook)
ISBN: 978-1-954201-09-5 (audiobook)

Publisher's Cataloging-in-Publication data
Names: Woodard, Tommy, author. I James, Eddie, author. I Gutteridge, Rene, author.
Title: Smells like bacon : The Skit Guys guide to lifelong friendships / Tommy Woodard and Eddie James ; with Rene Gutteridge.
Description: Rocklin, CA: K-LOVE Books, 2021.
Identifiers: ISBN: 978-1-954201-07-1 (hardcover) I 978-1-954201-10-1 (paper) I 978-1-954201-08-8 (ebook) I 978-1-954201-09-5 (audiobook)
Subjects: LCSH Friendship. I Male friendship—Religious aspects—Christianity. I Christian men—Conduct of life. I Christian life—Humor. I BISAC HUMOR / Topic / Religion I RELIGION / Christian Living / General
Classification: LCC BV4528.2 .W66 2021 I DDC 241/.6762–dc23

Book and Cover design by Charissa Newell II twolineSTUDIO
Cover photo by Dan Coronado

DEDICATION

This book is dedicated to Woody and Buzz, Bert and Ernie, Laverne and Shirley, Joey and Chandler, David and Jonathan, Laurel and Hardy, and all those who have loved a friend more than they loved their own soul.

CONTENTS

B.F.F.

FRIENDS FOR LIFE

"I have no idea how these
two made it as friends."

— MICHAEL W. SMITH

Grammy award–winning singer-songwriter and authority on friendship

The year was 1984. The setting was Edmond Mid-High. Eddie James, freshman football player and all-around moral guy, walked the hallways with the confidence of a sophomore, holding hands with his girlfriend, Jill. Every day held the promise of the blissful moment when Eddie would strut to the cafeteria, grab the hand of his beloved, and stroll down the hallway hand in hand with Jill, talking about their day. Perhaps some would call it puppy love, but to Eddie James, it was the most real thing he'd ever experienced in his life. She was indeed his everything.

Until one day—

Tommy: Wait, wait, wait. Stop. Hold up.

Eddie: What's the matter?

Tommy: This is the story we're starting with? To kick off our book on friendship?

Eddie: Yeah.

Tommy: This is a terrible idea.

Eddie: I think people should know.

Tommy: In my opinion, I think there are better stories to start with.

Eddie: Like what?

Tommy: Like the time I saved your life.

Eddie: You never saved my life.

Tommy: The time I introduced you to your wife.

Eddie: Didn't happen.

Tommy: The time I rescued you from that porta-potty.

Eddie: Stop. This is fine. Let the man continue.

Tommy: The man is us.

Eddie: What?

Tommy: We're the ones telling the story.

Eddie: Well, then, move aside and
let us talk.

—until one day, Eddie grabbed Jill's hand, and she didn't grab back.

Eddie tried again, but there was nothing. A quick glance at her body language told him there was a problem. A big, big problem.

Gathering his courage, Eddie stopped Jill in the middle of the hallway and said, "Hey, Jill . . . is everything okay?" Eddie looked deep into her eyes, the way he'd seen it done in all the John Hughes movies. "What's the matter?"

Jill took a breath and said, "Um . . . Eddie, I think we need to talk."

A chill ran up his spine. He'd heard of girls saying this to boys like him but had not yet experienced it for himself. Eddie swallowed hard but maintained his composure. "Okay. Let's talk."

"Eddie . . . I think I like someone else."

There it was, the emotional gut punch. All the breath left him.

As a steady stream of students rushed around them like water around a river log, Eddie grabbed Jill's hands. "Look," he said, "I can't tell you who to like, and I'm heartbroken that you don't like me. But I've heard about this one guy . . . this guy in the musical, and he has a bad reputation, okay? And so . . . so please, please tell me it's not that guy, that it's not—"

Tommy: It was me.

Eddie: Stop smiling.

3

Tommy: Tommy Woodard.

Eddie: Yes, you don't have to say your name.

Tommy: Some people might not know.

Eddie: That's how it all began. Tommy Woodard, master thespian and all-around jerk, stealing my ninth-grade girlfriend.

Tommy: I guess we have some explaining to do.

Eddie: I guess we do.

Tommy: By the way, I appreciate the "master thespian" tag, but "all-around jerk" is a little harsh.

Eddie: Harsh yet accurate. Tenth grade, you were a class-A jerk.

Tommy: True.

Eddie: A weird way to start a lifelong friendship, but that's how it started for us. Over a girl. A girl who later woke up, came to her senses, and ended up liking me again.

Tommy: Wait a minute—

Eddie: Not now. I'm finishing the story of how this closed chapter on a girl started an amazing chapter of friendship. We couldn't know then all the complications, laughter, hijinks, and common bonds we'd form in this

new chapter. But there you go—
lifelong friends because of a girl.

Tommy: Well, she didn't go back to you, did
she?

Eddie: Shhhh. Let's move on to defining
friendship.

What is a friend, anyway? This seems like a simple question. But in the digital age, where the lines between IRL (in real life) and social media are often blurred, maybe the question is harder to answer than it first appears.

Which is why we wrote this book.

Twenty or thirty years ago, we all took for granted our frequent, if not daily, interaction with friends, classmates, colleagues, and fellow churchgoers. But who (beyond a few extraordinarily perceptive writers and the God of the universe) could've predicted we would come to live in a society that struggles with social interaction and the formation of deep relationships?

Today, face-to-face human interaction is being traded in for the cheap counterfeits that digital media offers. And like an underworked muscle, we've begun to forget how to carry the weight and responsibility of relationship building.

We now struggle to know how to work out our differences, count on one another, build each other up. We're afraid, or maybe too tired, to reach out to our neighbors or answer the phone when a friend calls to talk (despite our phones always being at our fingertips).

In fact, many people might say it's just too hard to form deep and meaningful friendships outside our immediate families. Or that it's equally as hard to keep them, if we ever had them at all.

We wrote this book in the hope of inspiring you to blaze a new trail in the pursuit of relationships that exist beyond the screen. The kind that meets for coffee. That takes trips together. That writes letters of affection to one another. That picks up the phone to hear an actual voice.

Sound crazy?

Maybe it is crazy. But it's possible and also highly rewarding.

As we've found out in our thirty-plus-year friendship, the work that goes into building this kind of friendship is well worth the time and effort, because how it pays off is far more meaningful than anything you can ever find using Wi-Fi or an unlimited data plan.

Is friendship easy? Not always. But that's why we set out to write this book. We've learned a thing or ten over the years about having a good friend and being a good friend, and we wanted to share with you practical tips and nuggets of wisdom that apply whether you're male or female, young or old, married or single. We want to help you build relationships that you're more than willing to invest in, no matter the hills that need to be climbed. Sometimes the rockiest roads lead to the best of friends.

Finding and building friendships that last takes a little bit of courage. It requires you to take the risk of reaching out to say hello, to make the sacrifice of spending time you don't have, and the commitment to stay with the relationship through difficulties and hurts.

Does it sound daunting? Maybe it is. By pulling back the curtain on our friendship, we hope to show you that great friendship doesn't mean a smooth ride. You'll read about the anguish we've gone through as buddies. You'll hear about some of the misunderstandings we've had to crawl through together. But you'll also witness what this adventure has produced on the other side—and the harvest it still produces to this day.

We have a long track record, not of perfect harmony but of working out our differences and sharpening iron together. We have a feeling you'll be surprised by some of what you're about to read, but we hope you'll stick with us. You'll walk away with a new appreciation for friendship as well as the tools to build your own relationships to heights you never dreamed.

Buckle up!

— TOMMY & EDDIE

theskitguys

Letter written to my best friend
September

"why me God?"

I just feel so depressed. I feel like I don't know which way to go or turn. Everything seems so serious. I can't stand it! School is draining me. I'm already sick of kissing the teacher's butts and being there at every whim. I just wish things could be different. I started playing the "game"; now I want out. I'm not myself. So many commitments and none of them seem fun. I jus want some peace in my life. I've been struggling with my self-worth alot lately. I've been trying to find myself and alot of praying but it's good for awhile then it seems to get real bad, real quickly. I'm tired, so tired. I feel like something is on me...something heavy that I just can't lift and all I want to do is lift it up and leave it behind me. If I leave it behind me, I feel like could be losing something or hurting something or somebody. I'm not happy. All these names...President of this or the guy for this or in charge of that. They don't mean anything anymore. I want to be myself but something is holding me back. I want change but how does that come about? I know, I know leave it in God's hands. I'm trying but it just seems like things are going down instead of up. I just want to leave the past behind.

Eddie

*This letter was written to my best friend Tommy Woodard on the 16th of September. On the 17th of September Tommy took me to his church and there I gave my life to Jesus Christ. I've known about God and Jesus but I never realized he wanted to have a personal relationship with me through His son Jesus Christ. Tommy never got the letter but God heard the message loud and clear.
"Tommy, I owe you and love you!"

CHAPTER 1

YOU'VE GOT A FRIEND IN ME

"Friendship is so weird. You just pick a
human you've met and you're like,
'Yep, I like this one,' and you just do
stuff with them."

— *Often attributed to* BILL MURRAY,
but it's the internet, so who really knows?

n Mark chapter 2, a curious story emerges from the seaside town of Capernaum. Jesus is preaching in a local's house when four men arrive carrying their friend on a mat because he can't walk. They want to bring him to Jesus, but they can't get near the front door because of the crowds.

Put yourself in the sandals of one of these men and try to imagine the scene. It's crowded. Like, Black-Friday-at-Walmart crowded. Many are pushing and vying for the best viewing angle. A thick fog of humidity drifts in from the Sea of Galilee.

There are five of you. Four of you can walk, but one cannot. He's on a mat, so let's call him Matt. The details of how it happened aren't important, but the fact that he's dependent on other people has been a huge burden in Matt's life. You know your friend longs to be healthy so that he can fend for himself and care for his family like other men.

Today could be the day.

There's excitement in the air. The Rabbi is here. The One who heals. You heard whispers about Him a while back but blew it off as nonsense. But more and more people, claiming to be eyewitnesses, told you amazing stories of how this man makes the blind see and the lame walk. So when you heard this very man was teaching in a house just a few blocks away, you and your friends decided to take Matt to see the Teacher.

There are just a few hurdles to clear first. For one, you have no other way of transporting Matt other than a large mat that is unraveling by the second. Once you arrive, you're all out of breath because you're all out of shape. Yet here you are, Matt in tow, ready to witness a true miracle for yourself. For your friend. Then you realize there is no way to get to the Miracle Worker because a huge crowd is surrounding the house already. And that—

Tommy: Time out!

Eddie: It's a Bible story, not a football game. But go ahead.

Tommy: I just have to wonder if they were running late.

Eddie: For what?

Tommy: To see Jesus. That's why they couldn't get in. I don't know. Feels like everyone has that one friend who can never make it on time to anything.

[*long pause*]

Eddie: You're talking about me, aren't you?

Tommy: Why would you say that?

Eddie: Allow the man to continue.

Tommy: Again, the man is us.

You set down Matt and his mat under a shade tree. You wipe your brow as you look around at your friends. They're all exhausted. And now deflated. Hungry, too. Matt's gaze is fixed on the house, where people are crowded five deep against the outside walls, trying to get a glimpse through the window.

Matt stays quiet. He feels quite sure his opportunity has passed him by.

Let's leave Matt sitting there for a bit. We'll return to the scene—but you know, who doesn't love a good cliffhanger?

THE FOUR CIRCLES OF FRIENDSHIP

There's a scene in the movie *Meet the Parents* in which Greg, the soon-to-be-fiancé of Pam Byrnes, is desperately trying to win the approval of her father, Jack. Jack is wholly unwilling to give it, no matter how hard Greg tries. But when Greg inadvertently learns a family secret, Jack tells him, "With the knowledge you've been given, you are now inside what I like to call 'the Byrnes family Circle of Trust.'" What does that mean? As Jack explains, "I keep nothing from you. You keep nothing from me."

When we think about friendships, most of us instantly recognize that not all friends are the same. We use the word *friend* to describe an array of different levels at which we interact with people around us. We give a friendly wave to a stranger in the parking lot. We know a friend who has the scoop on game-day tickets. We call our friends to share good or bad news. We help a friend with a weekend project. We seek out friends at church to sit with them.

And then there's a whole new kind of friendship: social media friends. They "like" our pictures; we "like" theirs. We comment; they comment. There's a strange if nebulous bond that forms.

Even beyond that, there are the fictional friends we binge-watch every weekend when we're too exhausted to interact with real people.

Friend, it seems, describes just about everybody who isn't an enemy.

And perhaps that's not a bad lens through which to view those around us.

But being able to distinguish who is a real friend and who is not, and furthermore classify the different types of friends in our lives, will help us determine how we can best spend our time and energy in our relationships. We all know that time is one of our most valuable commodities in this world.

As keen social observers and longtime friends ourselves, we have categorized friendly relationships into four easily recognizable levels. We see these levels as circles, each one smaller and closer to us than the last.

Identifying which circle each of our friendships falls within is vital to maintaining the health of each one. Also, purposely cultivating each of these types of friendships can enrich our lives tremendously while creating a circle of trusted and treasured friends whom we can both pour into and receive from.

Let's take a closer look at each of the four circles.

The Acquaintance Circle
aka "Hey, How Are Ya?" Friends

This one doesn't need much explanation to define it, except to say that there are people you have to be with and people you get to be with. But it's worth noting that it is often with a person whose name we can hardly remember that an unexpected friendship can bloom. Likewise, it's easy to forget that a friendly acquaintance is not the person who is going to have your back in a crisis, and you shouldn't expect as much.

Folks in the Midwestern and Southern regions of the US sometimes struggle with this because of the friendly nature of the culture. We're raised to smile warmly at both our grandpa and the guy bagging our groceries. The pharmacist gets a "Hey! How are ya?" just like our childhood best friend.

The waters can get a little murky when we begin to confuse friendliness with a friend. That said, for the most part, all of our closest friends were at one time acquaintances. The stranger yesterday may be the newfound friend tomorrow. A coworker can become a cohort. Keeping an open mind toward the acquaintances in our lives, no matter how different they may seem, could mean gaining a potential lifelong friend if we give them a—

Tommy: Hey! I remember the first time I saw you, Eddie. It was in the Cafetorium. You were in *Annie Get Your Gun*, and at that point, I mean, you were just an acquaintance at best. And then my next memory is—

Eddie: I got kicked out.

Tommy: Well, you chose football.

Eddie: I got kicked out. I was a pretty big flake. I tried to do both football and theater.

Tommy: The ultimate theater sin.

Eddie: I was an idiot.

Tommy: You got better.

Eddie: Thanks. I like to think so. By the way, can we move on from acquaintances? This is the longest I've ever thought about acquaintances in my life.

Tommy: Okay.

Eddie: Seriously, are we writing a book about strangers or friends? When is the man going to stop talking about these no-name people in our lives?

Tommy: The. Man. Is. US!

Eddie: Then get on with it, man!

TRUE-FALSE POP QUIZ

1. True or False: I say, "Hey, friend!" to the Chick-fil-A staff in hopes of getting extra sauce packets.

2. True or False: I use the following verbiage because I'm terrible with names: "Hey, buddy!"; "Hey, pal!"; "Hey, bro!"; "Hey girlfriend!"; "Hey there!"; "Heeeeyyyy"; "Hey hey hey!"

The Hang-Out Circle
aka "Let's Grab Coffee" Friends

It's interesting in life how a mere acquaintance can turn into a Hang-Out friend, isn't it? And how certain moments, even bad ones, can shape an entire relationship.

One minute, she's the person you always see at the snack machine on the third floor, digging for change for that Twinkie she gets every afternoon at three o'clock. The next minute, she's invited you to her Bible study.

Or day in and day out, he rides the same bus to work as you do. Then you notice the book he's reading, and you strike up a conversation. A few weeks down the road, you've invited him to your basketball league (against your better judgment because you know your layup form breaks the heart of basketball fans everywhere).

Or a coworker breaks down and shares with you that he's going through a divorce. Months later, after a number of long talks in the break room, you've become friends.

It's always kind of weird, right? No matter how old you get, making plans feels like asking someone on a date, even though it's not a date: "Hey, ummm . . . you want to hang out Friday? I mean . . . yeah, I got a Groupon for two half-off tickets to AMC. If you're busy, you know, no big deal . . ."

But life can happen like that. We're all looking for those kindred spirits, aren't we? And isn't it amazing when we find them? It's such a joy to talk to someone who sees life the same way, who has the same interests we have, the same goals.

Hang-Out friends can enrich our lives in many ways. Often, they are just different enough from us that they offer new perspectives on life that we might never have gained on our own.

Hang-Out friends make us better conversationalists. Because we haven't yet developed the easygoing nature of closer friends, silent moments aren't always comfortable. We have to work a little harder to interact in these moments, which sharpens our relational skills.

Such friendships also cause us to become better listeners. If we're smart about it, these relationships should pique a healthy curiosity about the lives of others. As Dale Carnegie said, "You can make more friends in two months by being interested in them, than in two years by making them interested in you."

Tommy: You love Dale Carnegie!

Eddie: I do! I really do! That man influenced my life. And helped me win friends. You have anyone in your life like that?

Tommy: Fletch.

Eddie: Fletch? The, uh, fictional journalist in the 1980s comedy who goes undercover to break a story?

Tommy: [in his best Chevy Chase voice] "I'm afraid I'm gonna have to pull rank on you. I didn't want to have to do this. I'm with the Mattress Police. There are no tags on these mattresses."

Eddie: We'll charge it to the Underhills.

Tommy: Yes. Yes, we will.

Of course, Hang-Out friends have their hazards, too. The same friends who strike curiosity and spur adventure in you can't necessarily be trusted to have your back in an emergency or even want what's in your best interests. They won't hold you accountable, so they've also got the potential to plant destructive seeds in your life and lead you down some dark alleys. As is written in 1 Corinthians 15:33, "Don't be fooled by those who say such things, for 'bad company corrupts good character.'"

This circle is likely where most of our friends dwell. We're friends with them on Facebook. We know a few details about their lives. They're easy to talk to, and we'll always stop to say hello. We've been to a barbecue at their house and gained new respect for their intense love of ghost peppers.

Many will remain Hang-Out friends for all our lives, and that's okay. A heart has only so much room for the next two levels of friendship. But this level is a decent place to test the waters if you see a spark that might lead to something deeper.

#PROTIP

To make things less awkward when asking someone to hang out, eliminate the following phrases from your vocabulary:

X "No matter what you've heard, I'm not a stalker or anything like that."

X "Do you want to come over and see my stamp collection?"

X "I like my friends like I like my coffee—warm."

X "The voice in my head said we should be friends."

X "My max hug time is three seconds."

X "You ever wonder what went through Cain's mind before he killed Abel?"

X "If we become friends, I'll always be Batman to your Robin."

X "There are at least forty secrets to a lasting friendship. Sit down, won't you?"

The Circle of Honor
aka "Hey, Tell Me What You Think About This" Friends

This circle of friendship is perhaps the most intriguing of all of them. It's an in-between space. A special space. More personal. It's where you begin to dig deeper, where you wonder if this is a person who could really go there with you through the parts of your life that are sheer fun and the parts that are sheer pain.

One of the first signs that someone might be a Circle of Honor friend is that you begin asking his or her opinion. And not just asking, but valuing—

Tommy: Okay, hold up. Are we really going to call them Circle of Honor friends? 'Cause that sounds like your friend has passed on but you keep doing things to honor them.

Eddie: Who hurt you?

Tommy: Well, there's a whole list of people. But what does that have to do with this?

Eddie: Nothing. It's just a question I ask a lot. As to your question, it means that you honor their friendship. They are more than a Hang-Out friend but have not reached the apex of friendship with you.

Tommy: Well, with a name like that, it's no wonder they don't want to go the distance. How about calling them "Better Than Hang-Out Friends"?

Eddie: Too long.

Tommy: "Almost Apex Friends."

Eddie: Too dull.

Tommy: "Full-On Fantastic Friendly Friend."

Eddie: Now you're just being mean. Trust me, it's going to catch on. There will be T-shirts, a podcast—

Tommy: I don't think so.

You know you're onto something good when a potential Circle of Honor friend gives advice and it actually makes sense to you. Maybe you find yourself getting over your tough pride and leaning into that advice to the point of making a change in your life.

Maybe such a person is willing to say some tough things to you—tougher than anything you'll hear from your Hang-Out friends:

- "Hey, you apologize for a lot of things that don't even warrant an apology. You don't have to do that."

- "Do you realize you laugh every time we start to get into a serious discussion?"

- "When you were a kid, what did you want to be when you grew up?" And then they listen. And then it's, "I can see you doing that!"

- "Go ahead and get the bucket size. I know you love popcorn. No judgment from me!"

Okay, maybe that last one isn't great advice, but—

Tommy: And now we come to the bathroom story.

Eddie: Which is way more meaningful than it sounds.

Tommy: Traditionally, nothing great happens in a bathroom.

Eddie: True enough. But the situation was that you were a sophomore, and I was a freshman, and really my whole goal was just to beat you at your game because you stole my girlfriend. And I clearly had to get revenge, so I knew I had to get the lead in the play.

Tommy: I had no idea that's what you were doing.

Eddie: So we were in the bathroom. And at this school, the bathrooms doubled as the dressing rooms for our school plays. We were getting ready to go out there and perform, and I was so proud of myself for beating you out for the lead.

Tommy: You do know, I had NO idea that was your ulterior, cloak-and-dagger motive, right?

Eddie: It doesn't matter. It just matters that I won. So there we were, hanging out in the "dressing room," and we start joking around, making each other laugh. And I thought, *Why did I make him my "Johnny from Cobra Kai"?* That makes me Daniel LaRusso, by the way.

Tommy: I did feel like you wanted to put me in a body bag. But we were laughing and joking around, and there was this moment. We hadn't really hung out much, but there was this moment when I realized you'd accepted me as your friend. The initial, "Hey, buddy!" moment.

Eddie: YES! It felt like you noticed me. And I felt like I was doing funny stuff on my own and that I'd garnered a little respect from you.

Tommy: That's so fascinating because we were looking at it two different ways. I would've never thought of you like, *That guy's talented. I want to be his friend.* It was more like, *I like that guy, and I want to be friends with him. I want to spend time with him.*

Eddie: I was just waiting for you to see how awesome I was.

Tommy: As it turned out, you were awesome.

Here is where the commodity of friendship is important. You're making time, and you're giving time. How much is exchanged, and to what degree, is important to watch and consider. In this day and age, is there anything more valuable than time? If a Hang-Out friend is investing time in you and you find yourself making time for the friend in exchange, you eventually begin to realize that there's something special about this relationship that's worth considering.

Trust is also a commodity—one that we often keep in an emotional safe, only to be brought out in certain circumstances and with certain people. If you find yourself giving trust to this person, pay attention to that, too.

Circle of Honor friends should extend far beyond the world of social media. These days, entire relationships appear to be cultivated on social media, where people share everything from their dinner menus to their dark secrets. The wall of trust seems to have fallen, but what happens on social media can give us a false sense of relationship.

Circle of Honor friends have a more important, more prominent place in your life. You talk rather than text. You see one another in the flesh more often than on a screen. Because of this, in the family of Christian brothers and sisters, this special circle ought to be reserved (in most cases) for persons of the same gender.

A Circle of Honor friend is also someone with whom you're willing to sit in grief. You don't even have to know the details of the other's pain, but when you see this friend in pain, you hurt for them. Their pain doesn't pass you by without an acknowledgment. They may not even be able to tell you much about it, but they don't have to. You honor them with your time and trust, and that's enough.

Eddie: May I interrupt for a second?

Tommy: You're interrupting yourself, but go ahead.

Eddie: Sometimes we find ourselves trying with all our might to force someone into a circle they are never going to go to.

Tommy: Hard but true. Maybe they don't like you. It happens. And sometimes people can't give what they don't have.

Eddie: Yeah, we try to grab friends because we want them to like us. But we should mention that other people's opinion of us is none of our business.

Tommy: Right. We, of course, want their opinions and their thoughts of us to be good.

Eddie: But we can be consumed by that to the point of wanting to acquaint ourselves with them, hang out with them, and have them honor us.

Tommy: But it's futile.

Eddie: It is futile. Just thought that needed to be said. By the way, do you say "futile" fast, like it's a run-on sentence? Or do you break it apart, making the "tile" sound like it has the right to be its own state? [Eddie pauses to think and silently mouths the word to recall how he says it.]

Tommy: The latter. Can we move on now? Don't talk; we are moving on. Anything you say is fu-tile.

Keep in mind that the Circle of Honor is a place where deep betrayal can happen. But friendship is always risky. You have to put yourself out there and trust, and these are the folks you've chosen to surround yourself with because you've done your due diligence with them.

Circle of Honor friendships are the trickiest to navigate, but if you begin to see that you're having to convince someone to move to the next level of friendship, and they're just not willing to spend their time or attention, keep them in the Hang-Out or Acquaintance Circle. And remember, friends often move in and out of different circles. A coworker may become a Hang-Out friend for a while and then return to being an Acquaintance friend. A family member can move between circles, too. Unlike kids and teens, adults understand there's a certain level of trust you extend to each person around you, whether a coworker or family member. This trust is yours to give and yours to take away.

In addition, there are friends to whom you give honor despite not being able to spend much time with them. But they will always have your trust, and they will always have your time when needed. Distance or other circumstances might keep you apart, but you've extended honor to them no matter what.

Tommy: You know what I just thought of? Graduation. I chose not to go to any graduation parties. Instead, I went to the movies with you.

Eddie: With me, Stacie Bell, and Erin Cutter. And then from there, fast-forward to September—

Tommy: No! Don't tell them yet what happened in September 1987!

Eddie: I love that story! It's so important to our friendship.

Tommy: Everything in due time, my friend. Everything in due time.

Eddie: Okay, Gandalf the Grey. We'll wait.

READER POLL

Do you like "Circle of Honor," or is that a really stupid name?

☐ Love it—already made a T-shirt!

☐ Meh.

☐ Every time I hear "Circle of," it triggers the *Lion King* soundtrack.

The Garden Circle
aka "Let's Dig in the Dirt" Friends

The final circle of friendship is made up of what we call Garden friends. This name comes from the story of when Jesus was facing arrest, a trial, and crucifixion. He was distressed and asked His eleven disciples—by now, one had betrayed Him—to go with Him to a nearby olive grove. But from there, He took only three of those friends deeper into the garden with Him to watch and pray (Matthew 26:36–37).

Garden friends are those you're willing to go deeper with and till the ground alongside. There are few of these in your life. In fact, there can't be more than a few, as we'll explain later in the book. As we make our way forward, keep an open mind toward Garden friends. You may already have one or two in your life but don't know it. Maybe you know someone who could be a Garden friend, but you're unsure how to cultivate the friendship in a lasting way.

Garden friends constitute an important circle of friendship. These will be the friends you'll go to the moon and back for, the ones who will come over and dig a ditch with you. They're the ones who celebrate with you in your moments of greatest victory and stand beside you in your hour of greatest need—and call on you to do the same.

Eddie: I called on you once in an hour of need.

Tommy: Several times, yes. What are you thinking of?

Eddie: When I needed help getting some sand.

Tommy: I don't think that's exactly the same as what we're—

Eddie: I was a junior on the student council, and we were planning the senior prom. The theme was Egyptian. What's that Egyptian song by the Bangles where everyone walks around?

Tommy: "Walk Like an Egyptian."

Eddie: Yeah. We had tiki torches, and Stacie needed me to get sand. And I asked you to come with me even though you were a senior and it wasn't your job. That was a really cool buddy thing to do.

Tommy: She gave us some petty cash to get it. And then one of us realized that we knew where some sand was, and we could just get that sand and not have to spend the school's money.

Eddie: So we went to this place . . . this . . . what was that?

Tommy: A quarry. It's where Fred Flintstone and his pal Barney worked. We needed a lot of sand. Buckets full. So we went and got shovels, climbed the fence, threw the shovels over, got the sand, then loaded it all into my Chevette.

Eddie: And it should be noted, I hadn't said yes to Jesus yet. Still, I felt like I was a good guy. That was kind of my claim to fame: "Eddie's a good guy."

Tommy: Neither one of us were thieves. Like, that's not in our wheelhouse. Casanovas, maybe. But that day, it was total *Ocean's Eleven*. Well, it

was Ocean's Two. But what was done
was done.

Eddie: And so we had about thirty bucks. We
realized we needed to get some change
to give back.

Tommy: So that called for a trip to Sonic.

Eddie: An amazing trip to Sonic, my friend.

Tommy: We probably got double burgers, tots,
Route 44 drinks. And there may have
been some ice cream.

Eddie: Back then, they had the little
plastic monkeys and elephants that
came with the cup.

Tommy: So then we were able to go back and
say, "Here's your change." But then
Stacie said . . .

Eddie: "Where's the receipt?"

Tommy: "Where . . . is . . . the . . .
receipt?" At which point you were
talking, making up something, and I
fled the building.

Eddie: Yeah, you walked away.

Tommy: I'm hoping that the statute of
limitations has expired on that. What
were we talking about again?

Eddie: Garden friends, who don't leave you
in your hour of need. Our story
started strong but didn't have
the impact I thought it would for
this section.

Tommy: Yeah, at this point we're sand friends, making bad decisions together.

Eddie: We got straightened out.

Tommy: Thanks to Jesus.

BUDDIES + TOMMY'S CHEVETTE

Garden friends are hard to find. But once you find that kindred spirit, such a friend is worth keeping. How to keep a Garden friend and how to be one in return—well, that takes a special kind of attention, a tilling of the relational ground. And that's what we're going to explore in the rest of the book.

Cultivating a Garden friend requires a far look into your future and learning to play the long game. And that's—

Eddie: Wait, wait! We left the guy on the mat.

Tommy: What guy on the—? Oh yeah. Matt! We definitely need to finish that story. Let's see, we left them sitting under a shade tree and feeling defeated.

Eddie: Well, they didn't make it in time, so they might as well turn around and go home.

Tommy: That really could've been how it ended.

Eddie: Absolutely. But Matt had Garden friends.

Tommy: I mean, can you imagine the kind of friends you'd need to have where they're like, "We gotta do something for Matt"?

Eddie: And there's always that friend in the group, the one who's just a little bit crazy—

Tommy: And they already know the look in his eye, right?

Eddie: "Oh no, Toby has the look . . ."

Tommy: And there's the sensible friend, Jim, the one who is like, "Let's just talk to a few people and see if we can negotiate our way in."

Eddie: Then Toby blurts out, "WE'RE GOING THROUGH THE ROOF!"

Tommy: Now Jim's anxiety kicks in. He's never even had a parking ticket up to this point.

Eddie: And now Toby has hatched a radical plan to lower their friend through some guy's roof to get to Jesus. Gosh, I wish I could've seen that happen.

Tommy: And heard what all the people were thinking when they saw it.

Eddie: You need friends like that. Ones who will do radical things to get you to Jesus. I have a friend like that.

Tommy: I hope that's me.

Eddie: That's you. You prayed one night in September of 1987, and it changed everything! It was a dig-the-hole-in-the-roof moment in my book.

Tommy: Can't wait to tell that story later. And man, what an ending this story has in the Bible, when the men finally get Matt to Jesus, and Jesus sees their faith. We never really know the full impact Garden friends have on each other, do we?

POP QUIZ!

How does the story of Matt end?

a. The homeowners' association fines him $300

b. Roof digging is outlawed in Capernaum

c. Jesus heals Matt (and the Pharisees sweat a little upon witnessing the miracle)

AND... ACTION!

What is the first step to finding a good friend? We believe it's making sure you have the qualities of a good friend yourself. Take inventory of these four characteristics in your life:

1. **Integrity:** Are you trustworthy?
2. **Honesty:** Will truth be a pillar in your life?
3. **Empathy:** Can you allow yourself to hurt when others hurt?
4. **Compassion:** Will you give a friend the compassion God has given you?

Take a few moments to write down these four qualities and pray about them. Ask God to help you grow in each area. The stronger they become in your own life, the faster you will be able to identify them in the lives of others. Remember, like-minded people are naturally drawn to each other. When these qualities shine in you, others will take notice.

CHAPTER 2

CRYING AT BEACHES

L ike we said, good friendships require time and trust. A closer, deeper friendship is going to take more of each from both of you. How much are you willing to give? And how much are you willing to receive?

Have you ever been roped into participating in a trust fall exercise? Maybe at school, camp, or work? It works like this: You stand with your back to one or more persons—awkwardly if you're between the age of ten and puberty. The idea is to trust those behind you to catch you even though you have no real assurances they will.

Friendship, when it comes down to it, is a relational trust fall—

Tommy: "Relational trust fall"—is that the right term?

Eddie: Seems like it. Everyone's done the trust fall with friends at school or camp.

Tommy: Yeah, but it doesn't always go well, you know?

Eddie: I'm sensing a backstory with you on this . . .

Tommy: Oh, there's a backstory, all right. And a chiropractor story, too.

Eddie: I guess that's why they call it a trust fall. Not everyone can be trusted.

Tommy: Nor does everyone have the upper body strength they may appear to have. Besides time and trust, there is a third "T" that is useful in measuring the strength of a friendship. When offered, it can—

Eddie: Tattoos.

Tommy: What?

Eddie: That's the "T." Tattoos. If you want to take your friendship to the next level, get tattoos.

Tommy: You mean, like, get your friend's name tattooed on your arm?

Eddie: No, get matching tattoos.

Tommy: I believe the "T" word is transparency.

Eddie: What if I get "Skit" and you get "Guys" tattooed? And then when we stand next to each other, it will say—

Tommy: Guys Skit.

Eddie: I mean, yeah . . . if you're standing on the wrong side of me, I guess. Never mind.

Tommy: The actual third "T" is really cool, though.

Eddie: Just let me pout a bit.

Tommy: Okay, buddy. Okay.

So the third "T" is transparency.

Transparency doesn't necessarily require that both time and trust already be in place. But you want to be careful about being transparent with someone you haven't spent time with and don't trust completely.

We've all been in the awkward situation of barely knowing someone when they decide to spill very personal information that you don't feel qualified to handle with the care it requires. No time or trust has been invested in the relationship, so you don't know how to respond appropriately. In this type of situation, compassion is often all you can offer in return, which of course can go a long way.

But transparency is not just about telling each other deep and dark secrets. It's also about being who you really are. It's about dropping the poses and getting rid of the filters we normally use to make ourselves look good or strong or brave (or ripped or flawless or on vacation in Hawaii) and instead getting down to the nitty-gritty of who we truly are. In short, it's all about taking a chance and being vulnerable:

"I was so nervous at that meeting!"

"I've been feeling really sad about that situation, but I haven't told anyone."

"I was hurt."

"I feel—"

Tommy: —too vulnerable to tell this next story.

Eddie: Ooooh, that's a good one! Okay, um . . . I feel embarrassed eating barbecue in public. Your turn.

Tommy: I'm serious. Do you really think we should share this story?

Eddie: Oh, sorry! I thought we were playing the . . . never mind. Why wouldn't we tell the story?

Tommy: Did you catch what we just said about sharing too much, too soon with other people?

Eddie: I think our readers will be inspired by it.

Tommy: I think we may lose some hunters, linebackers, and extremely stoic women just by mentioning the movie *Beaches*.

Eddie: The year was 1989.

Tommy: Buckle up, friends. Here we go . . .

Eddie: I should mention that I was a freshman in college. You were a sophomore—

Tommy: That makes it even worse—

Eddie: —and we'd been hanging out a lot. We had some classes together. We'd sit out in the parking lot and talk.

Tommy: Or we'd go to breakfast.

Eddie: One night, we decided to go see this movie called *Beaches*. I think it was a Wednesday night. I'll check; I keep all the ticket stubs.

Tommy: You keep all the . . . wow . . .

Eddie: Well, for all movies. Not just the ones I see with you.

Tommy: But you're not a hoarder.

Eddie: No, no. So this was before the term "chick flick" was a thing, and this was a popular movie, and there was a song . . .

Tommy: In the theater that night are a few senior citizens and "women of a certain age."

Eddie: I've heard they like that term more than "middle-aged."

Tommy: And then there's you and me.

Eddie: We're definitely the only two guys in there. And the movie's unfolding, and we really didn't know much about it going into the movie . . .

Tommy: No.

Eddie: But the movie's about two women. Friends. One becomes a big star, and the other one is the dutiful friend who's always been there for her.

Tommy: "It must have been cold there in my shadow . . . to never have sunlight on your face . . ."

Eddie: Yes, it was. So we're watching this whole thing play out. And, like, it was a really good movie! But the ending . . . I mean, spoiler alert.

Tommy: Barbara Hershey dies!

Eddie: Not necessary, but okay.

Tommy: [getting misty] And she has a little girl . . . and . . . and Bette Midler decides to take care of her daughter.

Eddie: The movie ends, and everyone exits.

Tommy: But not us. We're sitting in complete silence. Not looking at each other. And weeping.

Eddie: We're trying to figure out how to leave the theater without being seen by anyone.

Tommy: We decide to slide out the fire exit to avoid the lobby.

Eddie: It's a cold night. January or February. We get to your truck, and we're both still crying. Just going, "You're my best friend!"

Tommy: "You're MY best friend!"

Eddie: "What if you died?" Just bawling our eyes out.

Tommy: "I don't know what I'd do without you!"

Eddie: It was an amazing feeling because I don't think I'd ever been that intimate with a buddy, with a guy.

Eddie: I think we even said to each other, "You're my hero."

Tommy: Yeah, we did.

Eddie: There really was something to it. It wasn't just words. There really was some fabric and concrete on that.

Tommy: The movie showed us what the reality could be, because *Beaches* is about a lifelong friendship.

Eddie: That's what we wanted, not even knowing yet that's what would happen. They started out as kids and were best friends throughout the whole thing. It's a great story.

Tommy: To anyone reading this who's decided that two men crying at *Beaches* is too much, I'd like to suggest that you skip the chapter on hugs.

Eddie: No, no, no! That's a good chapter! Plus, the tunnel of chaos stuff later is awfully bloody.

Tommy: Emotionally bloody, yes. The *Braveheart* of relationship development.

Eddie: Well, we've been transparent, anyway.

Tommy: It doesn't get much more transparent than admitting that, as college dudes, we cried at *Beaches*.

ACTUAL DEMOGRAPHIC BREAKDOWN
OF BEACHES TICKET BUYERS

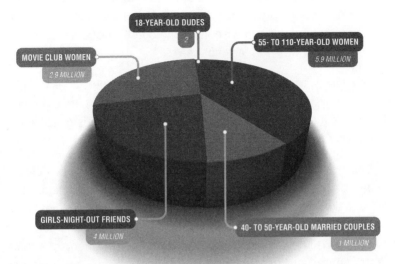

55- to 110-year-old women_____5.9 million

**40- to 50-year-old
married couples**_____1 million

Girls'-night-out friends_____4 million

Movie club women_____2.9 million

18-year-old dudes_____2

THREE TYPES OF TRANSPARENCY

There are several kinds of transparencies in life other than the unfortunate kind that happens when you buy white knit pants. When we practice transparency with wisdom and thoughtfulness, we can draw others to us in a way that "flexing" can't.

At a time when the average American spends hours on social media every day, the ability to put up walls and show only our best selves to others is incredibly tempting, even expected. But this rarely works out the way we're hoping.

Gazing at someone's perfect vacation photo, their fourth selfie of the day, or a beautifully lit shot of their perfectly staged devotional time hardly makes for a heart connection, which in the end is what we all crave. And we end up comparing what we know about ourselves to what we don't know about the lives of these "perfect" people. It really is the opposite of true friendship. True friends share the scars and scrapes of life along with the celebrations.

Recently trending on Instagram are "influencers" showing behind-the-scenes photos of what they really look like without Photoshop, filters, and lighting. As a society, we're all growing tired of the constant pressure to look and act perfect.

Still, it's one thing to post a not-so-flattering picture of yourself for the world to see. It's an entirely different matter to show someone a not-so-flattering side of yourself. Your true self. Your heart. Or to let your friend in when your house is a wreck, your kid is having a meltdown, or your marriage is falling apart.

Think about the word *intimacy* for a moment. Sound it out.

In . . . to . . . me . . . see.

In our special relationships, we allow people into the places we don't show to strangers or acquaintances. These are the places where things get messy. But it's where they also get really good. We love, and we are loved.

The urge is to show the world we have it all together. But the blessing is to have a friend who sticks closer than a brother or sister (Proverbs 18:24). So how do we do that?

Honesty

There's a great scene in *Beaches* when Barbara Hershey's character finally blurts out how jealous she is of Bette Midler's talent. "I can't even yodel!" she cries.

Nothing can ruin a relationship faster than a lie. Even casual Hang-Out relationships can be tarnished by withholding the truth. Lies, no matter how big or small, send a signal that we are untrustworthy.

But if we can commit to a life of honesty—both in how we portray ourselves on social media and to those around us in real life—we'll find that people will better relate to us. After all, they're human, too. However, before we can be honest with others, we have to be honest with ourselves. And finding our way down that road and through the deep forest of self-examination—that takes the Holy Spirit.

Most of us struggle with transparency and being honest with others because of fear: if they really know who I am, they might not like me. Because of fear, we fudge the truth, tell little white lies, flex our strengths one too many times. To build a friendship on fibs is like building a house out of straw and thinking the Big Bad Wolf can't blow it down.

In the end, when we decide to be honest, it's a relief to finally stop all those plates spinning. When we find the courage to say to another, "I'm kind of a mess," we've laid the groundwork for a relationship that's worth the investment. From there, the trifecta of time, trust, and transparency will pay off in ways we can't imagine.

2   Openness

Openness goes a step further than honesty. Openness means living your whole life without walls and having the willingness to give up closely guarding your image. The challenge with openness is that the older you get, the less natural it becomes. Children are great. They tell it like it is. They say how they're feeling. They'll let you know what they think of your jokes, your latest fashion choices, and your parking ability, all while not caring a bit what you think of them.

Since childhood, though, you've experienced a time when you were open with someone and it backfired. Maybe that person was less than receptive or just plain mean. It's happened to all of us. And the more it happens, the more walls we tend to put up.

What's the solution? Openness becomes easier the more open you are with God. Psalm 139:23–24 says, "Search me, O God, and know my heart; test me and know my anxious thoughts. Point out anything in me that offends you and lead me along the path of everlasting life."

As you begin to accept and, in fact, cherish an open relationship with God—not hiding who you are and what you struggle with, but instead allowing God to do the good work He promises He will do if you let Him—you will be better able to identify and anticipate the moments where openness will benefit both you and a friend.

#PROTIP

X If you're hit with a sudden urge to sing "Friends (Are Friends Forever)" by Michael W. Smith, don't panic. It's a reflexive response to pondering friendship. But sing with discretion. Once you start, this song will stay in your head for a long, long, long time. To remove this earworm, start humming a few bars of "Baby Shark." You're welcome.

3 Awkwardness

It has to be said: there's always going to be some awkwardness to living an open life. Vulnerability goes against the natural human tendency to protect ourselves. We'd love to say that it gets easier, but—

Eddie: It actually does get easier.

Tommy: It really does.

Eddie: When you decide you're going to be a fool for God, it starts coming naturally. But actually, you've kinda always been a . . .

Tommy: A what?

Eddie: Never mind.

Tommy: I've kinda always been a what? A fool? Were you gonna call me a fool?

Eddie: No . . . I was actually going to say that you've always been a wonderfully open person.

Tommy: We 100 percent just talked about honesty.

Eddie: Ugh. Friendship is tough. Fine, I was saying you've always been a fool.

Tommy: See? That wasn't so hard to do, was it? You were honest, and it felt good, right?

Eddie: We're going to talk about this later, aren't we?

Tommy: Oh, yeah.

The more transparent you are, even if you experience rejection now and then, the more you will come to understand how much your life, your realness, and your vulnerability can change the life of someone else.

Many of the people in your life are holding things in, believing they're the only ones who suffer from whatever it is they're suffering from. They feel alone. Many are afraid. Despondent. Hopeless, even.

By looking for moments to be transparent with people, you'll be amazed at the ministry opportunities that are created just with a simple conversation.

Tommy: I have to be honest with you . . .

Eddie: What now?

Tommy: Do you think anyone is still reading this?

Eddie: Feeling a little insecure, buddy?

Tommy: Maybe a little. Like, who are we to write a book about friendship?

Eddie: We're just two guys who, by God's grace, have been best friends for over thirty-five years.

Tommy: When you put it like that, it feels less heavy.

Eddie: I'm glad you told me how you're feeling.

Tommy: Now, about that "fool" thing . . .

QUICK QUIZ!

On a scale from one to "asking your boss for a raise," how comfortable are you confessing your sins and hang-ups to another person?

1. I have a standing confession on Facebook Live every Tuesday.
2. I eat ghost peppers, so I know how to sweat like a pro.
3. I practice in the mirror first.
4. I'd prefer to have my sock slip all day.
5. I'd rather ask my boss for a 50 percent pay hike!

AND... **ACTION!**

James 5:16 says, "Confess your sins to each other and pray for each other so that you may be healed. The earnest prayer of a righteous person has great power and produces wonderful results."

Who in your life can you trust to hear you confess your sins, faults, hurts, hang-ups, and habits? Talking honestly and openly with a friend is a great step toward healing personal wounds.

But before that, you must do some soul-searching to identify what your hurts, hang-ups, and habits are. Let's take a look at each.

These three terms are jargon used by Celebrate Recovery but can be useful to anyone, even if you're not in a recovery group. Because let's face it—we're all recovering from something to some extent, aren't we?

If you're ready, say, "Ready!"

You! Yeah, you with the Kindle. You didn't say "Ready." You just stared at the screen.

Okay, there you go. Let's dive in!

Hurts: A hurt is an offense that was inflicted upon you. You've likely carried it around for years. Many of us like to hold the hurt and even nurture the hurt. You can try sweeping it under the rug and pretending it didn't happen, but it never works. If you don't deal with the hurt, it will manifest itself and eventually grow into a hang-up.

Hang-Ups: These are quirky character defects like people-pleasing, anger issues, a need to control, or always having to be right. These are your Achilles heels, and they can really trip up your friendships. Maybe it's the way you compare yourself to others so you always end up looking better. Or the way you talk about others behind their backs. Or your need to be perfect. We all have them. The question is, Do you want to deal with them? Because if you don't, these little Mogwai—so cute and cuddly until they get wet—will one day turn into full-blown gremlins, aka habits.

Habits: Habits are little monsters that take over your life. Alcohol, gambling, porn, drugs, beauty obsession—whatever that thing is that so often determines your behavior. It's your bad habit. And as it grows, it will kill most of your relationships, including potential friendships.

If your hurts, hang-ups, and habits play a large role in how you function day to day, your relationships will suffer. And here's another word for you to think on: denial. Many of you may have read this list and thought, *My issues are nothing compared to most*. That's denial. It's not about most. It's about you and what kind of friend (or spouse or parent or mentor) you want to be.

Our hope is that as you learn these principles, you'll be better able to face the issues in your life that may be preventing great friendships from developing. Start by asking the Lord to help you prepare for and begin some enduring relationships. He is in the habit of blessing us with the things that matter in life.

> Jonathan was deeply impressed with David—an immediate bond was forged between them. He became totally committed to David. From that point on he would be David's number-one advocate and friend. . . .
> Jonathan, out of his deep love for David, made a covenant with him. He formalized it with solemn gifts: his own royal robe and weapons—armor, sword, bow, and belt.

— 1 SAMUEL 18-1, 3-4, MSG

CHAPTER 3

Don't Leave Me
at the Rodeo

One of the cornerstones of our friendship has been trust. When we describe some of our rules and boundaries, it might sometimes sound like an extreme form of trust. But it really is a foundation for how we're able to do what we do. Teaching, traveling, performing, having families, working together, playing together—all of it is built from a foundation of complete trust.

What does that look like from inside the friendship? What do we do practically to make sure we always maintain that foundation of trust?

Eddie: Okay, I'll start. It's Mesquite, Texas, circa 1990.

Tommy: Wow, that is gutsy! You're going to tell the rodeo story?

Eddie: Sure.

Tommy: I mean, I was thinking about it, but I spend every waking hour of my life trying to forget that story. But if you want to tell it . . .

Eddie: I do. As I was saying, We're in Mesquite. The air is thick with gritty dust and choking humidity. We roll up to the Rodeo Capital of the World.

Tommy: I mean, that's what the sign says. I don't think they can back that up with data.

Eddie: Anyway, we'd never performed in Mesquite, let alone at a rodeo.

Tommy: So we get there, and I don't know what we were expecting, but it wasn't that. It's an old rodeo barn, paint peeling like it's a hundred years old. We're going to be standing there in the arena, on this tiny stage in the middle of the dirt, and already we can tell this is going to be a disaster.

Eddie: Not the right venue for what we do.

Tommy: If there is one place that doesn't need skits, it's a rodeo.

Eddie: And the smell . . . oh, man . . .

Tommy: Then a horde of students comes in, clank clank clank echoing across the metal bleachers.

Eddie: Nobody has any idea we're there. Nobody's listening.

Tommy: But the mayor of Mesquite is going to introduce us, so we figure that's good. That'll get everyone's attention. And he comes up to us and says—

Eddie: Ooh! Do his voice! Remember his voice, all Texan and twangy?

Tommy: The reader can't hear us, Ed. It's a book.

Eddie: Could be an audiobook; you don't know.

Tommy: Trust me, they'll get it. So the mayor moseys over and says, "Howdy, boys. What do you want me to say about y'all?" We tell him one thing: "Just don't say we're the funniest guys in the world, because we know we're not."

Eddie: And he steps right to the microphone and says—

Tommy: "Here are the funniest guys in the world, The Skit Boys!"

Eddie: The Skit Boys.

Tommy: Smattering of applause.

Eddie: I think from the rodeo clown.

Tommy: Is that who the guy in the barrel was?

Eddie: I assume so.

Tommy: So we're digging out of a hole right from the beginning.

Eddie: I'm reading the room. Nobody is engaged.

Tommy: So we decide to do our best skit right off the bat. Every time we do this skit, it wins over any audience.

Eddie: Always grabs people.

Tommy: It bombed.

Eddie: Totally bombed.

Tommy: I'm sweating more than the farm animals. Meanwhile, there's another fifty people walking around finding their seats. Clank clank clank, like the sound of a rainstorm on a metal roof.

Eddie: Two twentysomething men talking should never be the first thing out of the chute at a rodeo.

Tommy: Yeah, we aren't a great appetizer. More like an after-dinner mint.

Eddie: We were just starting out, mind you.

Tommy: Not the confident speakers and writers we are today.

Eddie: Any-hoo . . . in a moment of sheer panic, I start setting up a skit.

Tommy: So I'm watching him and thinking, Oh, we're getting ready to do a different skit. Okay . . .

Eddie: I basically set up a monologue.

Tommy: And then he gestures toward me. I realize, *Oh no. I'm doing a monologue. He just tossed this whole thing over to me!*

Eddie: The whole enchilada.

Tommy: Now I'm up there playing a teenage valley girl, totally alone. There's the clank clank clank every time someone moves, the smell is choking me out, nobody is laughing . . .

Eddie: It should be said, Tommy gave a good performance. But then he finishes, and we have THIRTEEN MINUTES left.

Tommy: But wait, there's more!

Eddie: My mind is racing. What do we do, what do we do?! During the whole performance, I've been watching the crowd. No one is listening or laughing.

Tommy: And I'm drenched in sweat. I've just done an entire comedy set with no laughter. I can't feel my hands and feet, my vision is fuzzy, and . . .

Eddie: I pitch him into another monologue.

Tommy: "Here's a story about a boy named Dennis . . ."

Eddie: It's a very touching and moving piece he does about—

Tommy: Nobody cares! I carry the thing for another thirteen minutes by myself until the time mercifully runs out.

Eddie: I've gotta say, the feat was much more impressive than some cowboy riding a bull for eight seconds.

Tommy: Shut up.

Eddie: I thank the crowd and assure them we had as much fun as they did.

Tommy: I just walk off the stage.

Eddie: And that's when we had the talk—

Tommy: "We don't do that to each other. You don't leave me behind. That will never happen again."

Eddie: Yep, and it never has. We don't leave each other behind. We have each other's backs. Even when one of us is panicking and there seems no way out, we don't leave the other on a stage to carry the whole thing. And we don't leave the other stuck in a hotel lobby, talking to someone. We don't leave each other, period.

Tommy: I mean, life is like a rodeo, really. It can get dirty and hot and dangerous. Did you see those bulls that day? Terrifying.

Eddie: My friend, that day I made an oath to never leave you at the rodeo.

Tommy: And you never have.

Eddie: Of course, we never did a rodeo again.

Tommy: We're speaking metaphorically now.

As Proverbs 26:18–19 (NIV) says, "Like a maniac shooting flaming arrows of death is one who deceives his neighbor and says, I was only joking.'"

Friendship Killers

Betraying a friend's trust is like agreeing to back them up in a trust fall and then pulling away at the last minute and letting your partner fall on their keister. If it's ever been done to you, you know the wounds don't heal fast.

When you've entered into a friendship or a marriage, you've offered yourself to act as the other person's safety net. He or she is trusting you not to pull away.

The following are examples of actions and words that can kill trust—and therefore, a relationship—in the blink of an eye.

 ## Talking Behind the Other's Back

This can seem harmless enough. You might even think it's just a joke. But talking behind your friend's back about him or her can never be justified. It breaks trust. Even some mild gossip or a funny insult can prove damaging. It's easy to imagine how you'd feel if you found out your friend was talking to someone about you in this way. You might get a quick laugh with your comments, but you'll open up an unfortunate portal through which the devil can get an easy foothold. Resist the urge.

2 Dismissal

Some words are real verbal killers, and they can kill a relationship, whether acquaintance or spouse, with the flick of the tongue. If you make regular use of these words, you're guaranteed to find yourself in a lonely place.

When your friend is expressing how they feel—especially when they've been hurt—and you offer one of these retorts, it's like taking a knife to the heart:

"Give me a break."

"Oh, come on . . ."

"I was only joking!"

"I'm sorry you thought that."

"Whatever."

"Stop being so sensitive."

Dismissing someone's pain or hurt is a form of gaslighting, in which you dismiss the reality of the other person. Especially when this person is trying to express his or her pain to you, your dismissal can have grave consequences. The moment someone believes they can't trust you with their vulnerabilities, you've lost them, maybe forever. It takes a lot of work to win trust back.

Eliminate these phrases from your vocabulary. You'll be doing yourself a huge favor.

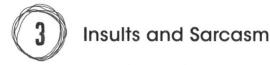

3 Insults and Sarcasm

We live in a biting, sarcastic culture, driven by barbs and needling in an attempt to get a laugh here and there. While that might work on a sitcom, all it does in real life is make you an untrustworthy friend.

A friend needs to know that you have their back. We trade fun barbs and insults on stage sometimes as part of our shtick, but you won't see us do it in a public forum outside our performances. We have each other's backs in all ways in real life.

That said, ours is a long-term relationship, and we enjoy driving the needle in here and there as good-natured fun. But we do it in private, not in public. Not only that, but if one of us needs to share some constructive criticism, that's always done in private as well.

There aren't many things more painful than to see a married couple insult each other back and forth, especially in public. Sometimes it's a passive-aggressive way they've developed to deal with problems. There's underlying tension that hasn't been resolved, so instead of hashing it out in private, one of them takes their issues public in hopes that the other person will catch on to the seriousness of the problem.

Insults and sarcasm chisel away at trust. This form of communication is also a form of bullying, and it never, ever achieves positive results. If you've done this in any of your relationships, go and apologize (especially if it's in your marriage). Even if you're not sure—say you like to trade barbs but wonder if you've taken it too far—go to the other person and ask for forgiveness. And if it's being done to you, ask the person to stop. It's never okay, under any circumstances.

There may even be no malice behind the behavior; it's pure insensitivity. But whatever the case, make sure you address it.

Not Speaking Up

As a general rule, we both know the other one is going to speak up on our behalf, whether we're in the room or not. If someone insults Eddie or talks bad about Tommy, the other of us won't join in and most likely will take defensive action on their behalf. Knowing someone will always speak positively about you does a great deal to strengthen a relationship.

By the way, this doesn't mean letting things slide. If you hear someone talking disparagingly about your friend, and there really is a problem that needs to be addressed, there's no reason you can't handle it privately later. The axiom "Praise in public, criticize in private" comes to mind. For instance, if someone at work is venting frustration over what a slob your friend is, leaving her trash everywhere, help pick it up and then maybe mention it to her later in private.

But when you know someone has your back through thick and thin, good and bad, it goes a long way. In fact, it can go a lifetime.

 Refusing to Give the Benefit of the Doubt

Have you ever been given the benefit of the doubt by someone? Maybe they heard that you said something about them and they've come to ask you? But instead of pointing an angry finger at you, they say, "Hey, I heard you said this about me, but I wanted to ask you directly because that doesn't sound like something you'd do." What a relief that is, isn't it, to know someone's first instinct is to believe you?

Of course, if you did say something, you can further strengthen the relationship by responding honestly. "Yes, I did say that. This was the situation . . . And I'm sorry. Will you forgive me?"

But any time there's a misunderstanding, giving each other the benefit of the doubt will always make a bumpy road smoother.

And withholding the benefit of the doubt can be harmful. Accusing a friend before hearing them out can only damage the relationship. We must be able to both receive and give the benefit of the doubt in a friendship.

A SHORT STORY
by Eddie James

One time, someone called Eddie and told him something that Tommy said. This didn't sound at all like something Tommy would do or say, causing Eddie's Spidey senses to tingle. Eddie, immediately sensing danger, did the only thing he knew to do: confront this person.

Eddie gathered his courage and said, "That doesn't sound like something Tommy would say," his biceps growing to an impressive sixteen inches as his voice echoed valiantly and his cape flapped behind him in the wind.

It was such a dynamic moment between the two of them that Tommy completely forgot about the rodeo incident.

The end.

AN EPILOGUE TO THE SHORT STORY
by Tommy Woodard

About 15 percent of this story is true. Someone lied to Eddie about what I said, and he confronted the person about it. In doing so, he actually turned down a really nice opportunity that could have been his. I am so deeply grateful he did that. It meant the world.

I still remember the rodeo.

And Spider-Man doesn't wear a cape.

The real end.

FRIENDSHIP BUILDERS

On the opposite end of the spectrum from Friendship Killers are Friendship Builders. These are words and actions that pump life into a friendship and equip it to last for the long haul.

Never Leave a Friend Behind

As we've mentioned, this simple rule applies to so many things in our friendship. We never leave the other guy stuck in the hotel lobby in a boring conversation while we slip away to the comfort of a quiet hotel room. We never leave one another hanging in a bad emotional state. We never leave the other to make a hard decision on his own, especially about the ministry or anything else involving what we do as a team. The list goes on. If one goes, the other goes. If one stays, the other stays.

2 Camaraderie

When two friends have mutual trust, it's a beautiful thing. But trust also must be closely guarded. One of the best ways to do that is to talk often about the camaraderie you have and enjoy. Even better, remind each other what it takes to keep that camaraderie going.

Recognizing and discussing the attributes and potential pitfalls of a strong friendship will keep everyone's eyes on the prize, and camaraderie is a prize indeed. But camaraderie is not something you just get to enjoy; it also must be cultivated. The more open you are about how to guard and protect it, the better the friendship will be.

It's not about "controlling" the relationship but rather taking the responsibility on yourself. You can periodically remind your friend, "Hey, I have your back. You don't have to worry about that." Or "I'm never going to speak bad about you behind your back. If I need to talk to you, I'll do it." These kinds of reminders will strengthen the bonds of friendship, and the favors naturally will be returned. This kind of attitude will inspire your friend to be a good friend in return. Friendship is built one trust-brick at a time.

Tommy: There's a story that sticks out in my mind about a time when you stuck with me even when it was super uncomfortable and even went against your nature.

Eddie: Oh, yeah?

Tommy: We'd agreed to do a gig as long as we could catch our flight that night to make it to another gig we had scheduled for the next day. All the details were laid out and agreed upon beforehand. But when we got there, the guy had switched everything around, making it impossible to catch our flight.

Eddie: You and I are pleasant people to work with. People need to know that. We bend over backwards and really try to accommodate folks. We are the Skit Guys, after all. It would be terrible if we were horrible human beings.

Tommy: That would make us very unfunny people.

Eddie: That said, we ended up having to work with a person who was very . . . how do I put this?

Tommy: A toot head.

Eddie: Okay. And Tommy, of the two of us, you're the laid-back one normally. But this guy was being pretty terrible about the whole thing. I mean, a big old toot head.

Tommy: When I hear you say it, it doesn't sound as awful as I want it to.

Eddie: I think everyone gets the idea.

Tommy: Anyway, we tried to reason with the person. Tried to be as flexible as possible. Tried everything. So we—

Eddie: Hold up. Whenever I think about this story, I see it in slow motion. Like a big battle scene in a war movie—a real do-or-die moment.

Tommy: I think I just said, "We're leaving," and tore off my mic.

Eddie: You did. But for a couple of comedians, that gesture may as well have been William Wallace in *Braveheart*. And I was kind of shaken because we'd never left any gig, ever, and we've been treated pretty badly in some places. But we've always stayed. We've always tried to "do the next right thing," so when you took off your mic, I was conflicted. Is this the right thing? Don't we have a contract? What will people say about us?

Tommy: But you followed me.

Eddie: Right out the door. Yeah, it was a literal mic drop. But I trusted you 100 percent. You stood up for us.

Tommy: I had to stand up to a guy who was disregarding everything that was right, you know?

Eddie: I do know, buddy. And I really liked how you slo-mo walked out of there, too.

Tommy: I'm pretty sure I just hastily exited out the back door.

Eddie: Not in my book, my friend. Not in my book.

---

3   Accountability

One of the very best qualities of a good and healthy friendship is built-in accountability. It's part of the idea that you never leave a friend behind. That includes when he or she is in a bad spot.

Accountability, of course, can prevent a lot of bad spots. We hold each other accountable in all kinds of ways, especially because we travel for work and are away from our spouses much of the year. Traveling with the person who is most likely to keep you accountable is a nice perk.

But accountability goes far beyond keeping an eye on one another. It also means keeping an eye on yourself. And when you've failed yourself, you've got to go to your accountability partner and confess it.

As an accountability partner, your job is to hear and respond with grace, love, encouragement, and a good measure of strength. You've now been put on high alert to keep watch over your friend in a place of confessed weakness. This includes prayer and lots of it. There's no judgment, but there is vigilance. Among other things, you've chosen to walk the straight and narrow together, side by side.

ACCOUNTABILITY MISFIRES

Phrases to never use when someone comes to you to confess:

X I knew it! I knew you would fail! I had bets going on it.

X I actually already knew thanks to that Handy-Cam I bought on Amazon.

X Oh, that silly sin? Forget about it. No biggie.

X Well, in terms of the scorecard I'm keeping, we're now pretty even on mess-ups.

X I've got some punishment ideas already lined up, my friend.

1. **Get the Friendship Killers out of your vocabulary.** There's no room for them in any friendship. It's degrading and humiliating to the other person. Just get rid of them.
2. **Spend time expressing to a friend or partner the ways your bonds can be strengthened.** And let them know what you're willing to do to make those bonds stronger.
3. **Make a commitment to yourself and to God about the kinds of behaviors you're going to begin to implement to become a good friend.** Write them down. Remember, the best way to gain a good friend is to be a good friend. It's never too late to start.

CHAPTER 4

WHY DON'T YOU HUG ME?

bet if we asked, many of you could quickly identify one or more friends in your life you absolutely love, yet the relationship constantly teeters on the edge of a cliff. These friends are fun. They fill a void in your heart. You would even say they have huge significance in your life . . .

As long as you don't rock the boat.

As long as you keep the peace.

As long as you keep your opinions to yourself.

As long as you keep it light and never too serious.

As long as you don't make a big deal about it.

As long as you just have fun together.

As long as you don't ask hard questions.

Do you have a relationship like that? That if you said what you're really feeling, the friend might walk away and never come back? And so you decide you'd rather have a shallow relationship than no relationship at all?

Or maybe you have a friendship like this: they run hot and then cold, leaving you confused. They're kind of like a cat—one minute you're the center of their world, and the next minute they're looking for Friskies cat treats somewhere else.

Sigh. So many relationships tend to linger in this category. We enjoy them, but they have their limits. Or we think they do. The truth is, we're afraid to know what those limits are; we're afraid to test them.

Perhaps you have another friendship that is extremely one sided. Your friend is happy to share his or her opinions about everyone and everything but are unwilling to hear anything you have to say.

Maybe you have a sense that you have more affection for the person than he or she has for you. However, after weighing the pros and cons, you decide you're okay with maintaining the imbalance as is.

But . . . what if you didn't?

What if you didn't settle for where the friendship is but instead asked more of it?

Is it wrong to want more out of a friendship? Or should you just take what you get and don't throw a fit?

Eddie: We have a great example of this, don't we? It was the spring of 1989. We were about to leave to serve as interns at a church in California. We'd been working out a lot to build our beach bodies.

Tommy: We skipped college classes to work out. That's how dedicated we were.

Eddie: Or to go eat big sausage-and-gravy breakfasts.

Tommy: I miss my college metabolism.

Eddie: Let me start by saying we come from two different types of families. You come from a very loving, hugging, verbal-type family. My family was very closed off at that time—maybe it was the stress of raising two teens

and a baby in the '80s. We were
preoccupied more with making ends
meet than meeting each other's unmet
needs. We loved each other, but it
was more like, "hugs later, survive
now."

Tommy: "You know I love you, and if it
changes I'll let you know."

Eddie: Exactly. So one night after working
out, we were in your truck, and you
wanted to talk. I remember you were
"angsty."

Tommy: I don't even know what that means.
But there was something that had been
bothering me . . .

Eddie: That's what it means. You were
clutching that steering wheel with
sweaty hands and white knuckles like
a little girl driving a getaway car
in a *Fast and Furious* movie.

Tommy: Because I'm about to say something to
you that a friend doesn't really say
to a friend, right? And I'm afraid
I'm going to ruin the relationship.

Eddie: I'm literally just sitting there
like, "Yeah? What? Just say it.
What?" And you're stammering
and staggering.

Tommy: And then I just blurt out, "Why don't
you hug me?"

Eddie: Just like that. And I said, "Uh . . .
what?"

Tommy: Because you were like a dead fish when I'd hug you. Your body would just go limp. I'd come in for this huge bro hug, like, "Hey, see you later!" And you'd just hang there—

Eddie: So I reply, "What are you talking about? Of course I hug you."

Tommy: And I'm trying to explain. "No, you don't! When I go in to give you a hug, you don't hug me back." And you're like, "What?" So I repeat, "You. Don't. Hug. Me. Back."

Eddie: So we go back and forth in a debate that no two dudes ever have on how to hug. Am I doing it right, etc. Finally, I say, "Huh. Okay. Well, I guess I'll hug you back." I had put up this wall to keep anyone from getting too close, but this was the first time I'd ever been confronted about it.

Tommy: It was a Proverbs 27:17, iron-sharpens-iron moment. We just didn't realize it. You could have blown it off. No one would fault you if you said, "Dude, that's dumb." But you didn't. You at least listened and received it.

Eddie: You know today, I hug my kids, I hug my wife, I'll hug a friend or someone who's hurting, and I'll think, *Tommy taught me this*. And it all started with an angsty conversation in a truck.

Tommy: A conversation with a little girl with sweaty hands clutching the steering wheel of a getaway car.

Eddie: She was a pretty smart cookie.

Friendship Blue Book: Know Its Value

Being able to say the hard things to a friend is a good measure of how valuable the friendship is to you. And once that ice is broken, once there is room for talking about the hard things, it's amazing how the friendship can grow and blossom from there.

But somebody has to have the courage to say it, and the other person has to have the courage to receive it. No matter how awkward it may feel to "be in the truck" at that moment, if you will try to hear what the other person is saying and reject the urge to react negatively or get defensive, you could strike gold. It's about responding rather than reacting.

Remember this: If someone is taking the time to say a hard thing to you and has mustered up the courage to say it while bracing themselves for the impact it might have, don't you think that person must find you valuable? Why would they go to all the trouble to have an angsty conversation if they didn't think you're worth it? Yet many worthwhile friendships have died on the side of the road, so to speak, because one person could only interpret an angsty talk as a negative confrontation.

If you're the person brave enough to start the conversation, you know you're running the risk of being brushed off. So wait a few days, if necessary, for the other person to fully respond. We all need a little time to process sometimes, but there are a few personality types who are not fans of conflict and might interpret what you're saying as aggressive or upsetting. Once you've said it, don't force a response. Give them space to consider what you've said.

It's Okay to Need More from a Friend

If you find yourself being unable to express what you need from a friend—or find them unable to hear it—you've got to come to the harsh realization that this person is not really a friend. At least not the friend that you need.

And it's okay to need more from a friend. It doesn't mean you're needy. It just means you've got to find a person who has the same life goals as you.

A friendship, by definition, can't be one-sided. So take stock of your relationships. Take their temperature. See how healthy or sick they may actually be.

And if you find yourself on the receiving end of the angsty conversation, like Eddie, then take to heart the advice from the apostle: Be quick to listen. Be slow to speak. Be slow to anger (James 1:19).

Once this dynamic is formed between two friends, it can spark something you'll never regret.

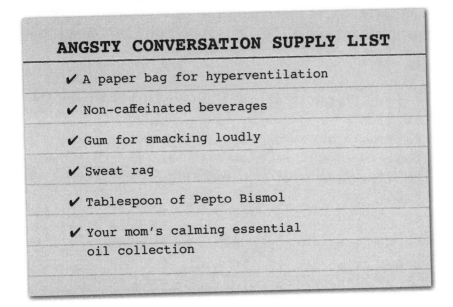

ANGSTY CONVERSATION SUPPLY LIST

✔ A paper bag for hyperventilation

✔ Non-caffeinated beverages

✔ Gum for smacking loudly

✔ Sweat rag

✔ Tablespoon of Pepto Bismol

✔ Your mom's calming essential oil collection

The more these kinds of conversations take place, the easier they become. The angst diminishes, for the most part, and the push and pull becomes woven into the fabric of the relationship. In other words, it begins to occur naturally, much like the brilliant rapport between Abbott and Costello.

Having the courage to ask for more or point out a problem generates respect and even trust between friends. And when trust and respect multiply, friends become inspired by each other's good traits and want to implement them in their own lives. Together, your differences can create magic.

Ridding the Relationship of Rejection

A mere whiff of rejection can stop us dead in our tracks when it comes to bringing up hard subjects. Rejection is the dismissal of a person or idea, and no one wants to feel dismissed. Face it: we've all felt that feeling.

Even so, to "go there" is everything we were created for. We need people. God set it up so that we need one another and then commanded us to love one another as we love ourselves.

Still, we often stop dead in our tracks out of fear that a friend—or worse, a spouse—might turn their back on us because we are too much to take. Anxiety lives in the gap between what we have and what we fear. Most of us sweat just thinking about asking the tough questions, much less confronting them.

But we must. We need to know who those next-level friendships might be with, whatever the question is.

"Why don't you hug me?"

"Why does anger seem to be your go-to response to problems?"

"Your dad's death wasn't your fault, but you live like you're still trying to win his approval."

"I seem to tell you many things in my life, but when I ask you, you always say, 'Things are fine.' Are they really?"

"You are missing details, and that's not like you. What's going on?"

"Hey, how's your heart? If God doesn't look on the outward appearance but looks at the heart . . . I just feel compelled to ask."

If we are to experience deeper love in friendships and relationships, we must take some baby steps of faith to see if the other person is willing to go there. Or as Ross on *Friends* says, "Pivot! Pivot!"

Tommy: There are unspoken things that, through the years, each of us has seen in the other person. We don't say, "I need to start doing that." I just like what you're doing, and I start doing it too.

Eddie: Even minuscule things like, "Hey, bring your running clothes to the gig. We're going to go run five miles." Iron sharpening iron. Making each other better. You think about all God did in that truck.

Tommy: That's why that Rich Mullins song means so much to us.

Eddie: Yep, "What Susan Said." About "two lonely-eyed boys in a pick-up truck."

Tommy: Driving through rain and heat and, in Oklahoma, tornadoes. It's like the song was written for us.

Eddie: It's the epitome of what we're trying to do with skits—not making them cheesy but more like *SNL* meets the Bible, right?

Tommy: Yeah.

Eddie: I remember our first gig that wasn't for a chicken dinner and gas money. We actually got paid.

Tommy: Like, 200 bucks each. It was fantastic! And we're thinking, *We can do this for a living!*

Eddie: I've got plans to buy CDs with my share, and I ask what you're doing with your money. And you mention you're going to tithe first and then give some money to your sister. I thought, *Why would you do that?* And I think I asked what a tithe was.

Tommy: I explained that I was going to toss in at least twenty bucks at church.

Eddie: I didn't even want to get into "at least." But it was a great moment. You weren't teaching. You were just doing what you were going to do.

Tommy: That's always been the trajectory throughout our friendship. I'm pretty much always being content with where I am, but I'm thinking, *Eddie's always working and bettering himself. I can better myself too.*

Eddie: But you've also taught me to learn to relax. Be content.

Tommy: Looking back over our friendship, there have also been negative times when we weren't balancing ourselves. We were in our early thirties, and we were going to buy two pizzas after every show—

Eddie: Larges.

Tommy: —and a cheesecake.

Eddie: Because we deserved it.

Tommy: Because we deserved it.

Eddie: Together, we easily reasoned that we could each consume a large pizza.

Tommy: Meat lovers and a liter of Coke. Why not?

Eddie: We needed it.

Tommy: We needed it. We deserved it. Those were our "chubby buddy" days.

Eddie: Oh, man, those were good days.

Tommy: I couldn't breathe after walking upstairs, but those were good times.

✎ HOMEWORK ASSIGNMENT

Rent an old pickup truck. Play "What Susan Said" by Rich Mullins really loud with the windows rolled down. Have a few angsty conversations with your passenger. Tell lots of stories about it later.

How to Start and Finish a Confrontational Conversation

1. Always pray about it. Ask the Lord if confronting this person, no matter what it's about, is in His will. And ask for grace.

> *Example of how not to pray:* "God, you probably don't want me to do this, so I won't."

2. Examine your own motives. Make sure that the confrontation is not selfishly motivated but, rather, motivated by a desire to help this person or the friendship in some way.

> *Example of a selfish motive:* Roger has a lot of money. The least he could do is pay for dinner.

3. Be prepared to pivot if the timing isn't right.

> *Example of bad timing:* Tornado sirens are going off.

4. Be okay if the conversation is initially rebuffed.

> *Example of how not to handle a rebuff:* You flip the table over and stomp off.

5. Don't be afraid to revisit the topic at another time if you feel it needs to be addressed.

> *Example of not revisiting it:* "Oh well."

6. If the conversation is received, thank the person for listening

> *Example of thanking the person:* "Hey, thanks for listening. I appreciate it."

How to Receive a Confrontational Conversation

1. Try to listen and really hear what the person is saying. Even if you feel the need to defend yourself . . . don't. Just listen.

> *Example of defensiveness:* "Stop talking. You're wrong. About everything. Since the day you were born."

2. Ask questions if you need clarification. Ask for examples of what your friend is talking about. "Help me understand" is a great, nondefensive place to start. When the other person feels noticed and seen and heard, the relationship grows.

> *Example of an unhelpful question:* "Did you dress yourself this morning?"

3. Tell the person you're really going to think about what they're saying. Then take time to consider and pray over the conversation in the following days.

> *Example of unhelpful pondering:* Thinking, *Betsy's lost her everlasting mind. I was always worried she would. I should confront her about that.*

WHAT TO DO WITH IT ALL

Being able to ask for what you need, and hear what someone else needs, is a sign of a growing friendship. Thank God for the friendship, and ask Him to continue to grow it. Inviting God into a relationship will do wonders for it. He is able to fertilize it in ways we aren't, and when God's involved, great things are sure to happen.

AND... ACTION!

Think of a friend you need to have a con-versation with. Write a letter to that person to help you gather your thoughts so you know what you want to say. Then pray about how you might approach your friend, and broach the subject.

CHAPTER 5

Keep Your Hands and Feet in the Goose at All Times

In the movie *Parenthood*, Steve Martin's character, Gil, is interrupted during a rant about how messy and unpredictable life is when Grandma suddenly appears and begins talking about the time Grandpa took her on a roller coaster and how it made her feel scared and sick but also thrilled and excited. Grandma seems to be babbling about a random memory, so Gil waits and politely listens. But then Grandma says that some people didn't like the roller coaster; they went on the merry-go-round instead. "That just goes around," she says with a twinkle in her eye. "I like the roller coaster. You get more out of it."

There's a term we use within our friendship: Tunnel of Chaos. It's about as fun as it sounds. In short, we use the term to describe when one person needs to confront another person about something extra difficult, knowing up front it may not go well and may require intense effort to get through. It's not seeking out chaos. It's seeking out clarity. But the expectation of getting to that clarity is similar to how you feel riding a roller coaster. Not just any roller coaster but something like Space Mountain, where you're rocketing through pitch-black darkness. Or the Texas Giant at Six Flags, the wooden roller coaster where you hear every creak and moan of that contraption for three and a half heart-pounding minutes.

To put it in another, less terrifying way, the tunnel of chaos is the ornery little brother to the Tunnel of Love. We're all familiar with the tunnel of love. Two people sit in a boat shaped like an oversized goose, drifting along a lazy river, sharing lighthearted talk, and—

Tommy: I think it's a swan, isn't it?

Eddie: No, it's a goose.

Tommy: But swans are more elegant. Like, a goose can kill you, can't it?

Eddie: We're going with goose. It's a goose. I've been on one. It's totally a goose.

Tommy: Okay . . .

In life—in real life—in order for anyone to get to the tunnel of love with a friend, spouse, family member, or even coworkers, sometimes we must go through the tunnel of chaos. It's not as fun or romantic as the tunnel of love, but it does propel us forward toward love.

In other words, the willingness to confront, to talk about hard things, opens the door to communication, making it possible for two people to work out their differences. We are all human, and we are all different, so naturally, doing life together gets messy.

So buckle up, strap in, and keep your hands and feet in the goose at all times because this will inevitably be a bumpy ride.

Tommy: Remember that time—?

Eddie: No.

Tommy: You don't even know what I was going to say.

Eddie: Pigeon Forge.

Tommy: Okay, fine. We don't have to tell it.

Eddie: Of course we have to tell it. You brought it up, so everyone is going to be demanding it now. They'll hold up the whole book until we tell it.

Tommy: I don't think that's how books work . . .

Eddie: Here's the gist: We go to do the bungee jump off a bridge in Pigeon Forge, Tennessee. Tommy takes the plunge, no problem. Then it's my turn, and I'm busy calculating my chances for physical survival versus the likelihood of my self-esteem surviving if I back out. All these strangers are behind me, chanting, "You can do it!" But I can't do it. I back out, and then I convert it into a whole life-evaluation thing. You know, you're not a success because you didn't conquer it.

Tommy: Whereas I can bungee jump, but I try to avoid the tunnel of chaos at all costs. I hate conflict!

Eddie: We are totally the opposite. I can do emotional conflict, but I couldn't bring myself to jump off that bridge.

Tommy: But we did do the Slingshot together. That ride pulls you backward inside this ball and then lets you go, like a slingshot, shooting you into the sky. The two guys in charge of the ride are strapping us in, giving us all the safety instructions—keep your hands and feet inside the ride and all that—and then they ask, "Are you ready?"

Eddie: I'm nodding yes but feeling no.

Tommy: Then one guy starts the countdown: "Three, two . . ." And here's where they get cruel.

Eddie: Yeah, this was unnecessary.

Tommy: Just before he gets to "one," the other guy starts shouting, "Wait, wait, wait!"

Eddie: Said with the kind of alarm in his tone that makes you think he noticed some bolts have fallen off . . . but he's too late. We're launched!

Tommy: And all I can hear are my own screams and the words "wait, wait, wait," and I think, *This is how I'm going to die. How will I explain this to my wife?*

Eddie: Then the bands catch us, we start drifting back down, and I realize we're going to be okay.

Tommy: That's the carnival ride equivalent of the tunnel of chaos. You're going into it, and everything is telling you, WAIT, WAIT, WAIT! DANGER! I DON'T WANT TO DO THIS!

Eddie: But it's a complete thrill once you come out of it, because you know something really amazing has happened.

Tommy: And you're just so happy you haven't soiled your pants.

Eddie: You know, maybe we should've started out with a different example.

Tommy: What do you mean? That's a great example.

Eddie: But we might've freaked people out. Listen, everyone, keep reading. Don't worry. We have professional-grade tools for your Batman utility belt to use when you're in the tunnel of chaos.

Tommy: We mixed a lot of metaphors there, but since you're already knee-deep in it, I'd say, "Yes, we do!" Because there's nothing worse than being stuck on that love goose with the Joker!

Eddie: Personally, I think there's nothing scarier than an angry goose. Their wingspan is terrifying!

THE TOOLS

The tunnel of chaos can open in any number of ways. But surviving it—well, that's the tricky part. It's also the most rewarding. It deepens friendships in ways that just floating along on the surface cannot. That said, going through the tunnel without the right tools at hand can make it difficult, if not impossible, for the friendship to emerge better for the experience.

Notice here that we've said tools, not weapons. This isn't warfare. If you go into it with that mindset, you'll both be coming out bloody. Tools fix things, and ultimately, the tunnel of chaos fixes things on the other side.

Here are a couple of tools or principles that will help you through it.

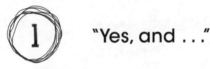 **"Yes, and . . ."**

The phrase "Yes, and" comes from the world of improvisation, where it's also known as the acceptance principle. The "yes" means that when one person in an improv scene makes a statement, his or her partner in the scene starts by accepting the statement as truth. The "and" part of the equation then kicks in, meaning the partner builds on the reality that's been established.

If you've ever seen good improv in person, you know it can be a pretty magical experience. One person begins the scene, setting the reality, and another goes along with it, thinking quickly on his or her feet to propel the scene forward and (hopefully) provoke laughter from the audience.

In much the same way, a friendship works on the "yes, and" principle, meaning there must always be forward momentum propelled by giving and accepting in a continuous effort to keep communication going.

In a relationship, if you're not giving something extra but rather shutting it down by refusing in a sense to accept the reality in front of you, the relationship is going to die. In the Skit Guys' world, most people see only the harvest of our friendship—the fun, the good, the strength. But it's behind the scenes, so to speak, where the real work is done.

If a friendship is a garden, it's the work in the dirt that keeps it alive. And that is where the tunnel of chaos happens.

THE HOTEL DILEMMA
A Cautionary Tale of Avoiding Conflict (CliffsNotes Version)

Setting the scene: An ordinary
hotel room

The participants: Tommy and Eddie

Time: Night

Tommy's Hotel Habits:	Eddie's Hotel Habits
✔ Lock the door	✔ Maybe lock the door
✔ Hang up all clothing	✔ Toss clothing everywhere
✔ Use clippy hanger to clip curtains together	✔ Find light comforting
✔ Put towel against door to block all light	✔ Pick TV show to shut brain off
✔ Cover alarm clock to block light	✔ Fall asleep with TV on full volume
✔ Burrow under the covers in complete silence	✔ Wake up when roommate tries to grab the remote and turn off TV
	✔ Refuse to turn off TV because "I'm watching that"

The dilemma: They don't share hotel rooms well.

The duration: Eight years.

The solution: Talk to each
other about it.

The reality: They never
talked about it.

The lesson: Don't suffer through it.
Talk about your problems.

Tommy: The tunnel of chaos was something we had to find our way through, learn how to do together.

Eddie: Yeah, we didn't always do it in a healthy manner.

Tommy: There were whole stretches when we simply didn't confront problems.

Eddie: Eventually, we figured out it was okay to ask for separate hotel rooms when we book a gig.

Tommy: Changed my life—eight years later.

Eddie: All those years, I'm completely oblivious to any of your needs.

Tommy: And given my personality, I don't want to be a problem, so I don't say anything.

Eddie: But you did confront me over the late-night movie runs after a gig. It would be, like, 9:30 at night, and I'd insist we catch a movie.

Tommy: And so we'd go, and you'd fall asleep.

Eddie: Totally out. And then I'd wake up and not understand the plot at all.

Tommy: And you'd sit there and make fun of the movie because none of it made sense to you.

Eddie: It's amazing how dumb a movie can seem if you miss some of the more important plot points.

Tommy: And so finally I confronted you about it. "Hey, buddy, every time we go see a movie, you fall asleep. And I'd rather just go back to the hotel and sleep."

Eddie: And I say, "No, no. I'm good. I won't fall asleep. I'm wide awake. Come on, let's go see it."

Tommy: I fold, and we go see the movie. And when I look over—

Eddie: I'm totally asleep.

Tommy: Finally, I just had to say, "I don't want to go to the movies. I want to go back to my room."

Eddie: And I didn't want to go back to the hotel and just sit.

Tommy: One of us wasn't getting what he wanted.

Eddie: But those are the "yes, and" moments. We keep going, whatever the reality.

Tommy: The tunnel of chaos is like broccoli to me. I used to hate the stuff—avoided it at all costs. But I have friends and family members who love broccoli and can't get enough of it. So I started making myself eat it. Today, there are times when I'll eat it in a salad and think, *That's not so bad.* Other times, I'll take a bite and think, *Just keep eating it. It's good for you. I doubt I'll ever love broccoli, but I will keep eating it.* The tunnel of chaos is good for you. It's healthy for your relationship. So you ride it when you like it and when you don't.

Eddie: Wow. That's a great analogy. Did you just come up with that?

Tommy: Right on the spot.

Eddie: BAM! Mic drop. Except with a cruciferous vegetable.

Tommy: You just killed the moment, but it's not your fault. Broccoli kills a lot of good things.

2   Iron Sharpens Iron

Any time you have to confront a friend about anything, there is going to be a certain level of discomfort. The hope is that you'll eventually come to a place where when someone says, "Hey, I need to go through the tunnel of chaos with you," you don't immediately bristle and back away. But that's probably not realistic. Rather, your posture should be that while you don't necessarily look forward to it, you can look it in the eye and think, *Okay, this may be challenging, but I know we're going to get through it.*

The important thing about maintaining a healthy relationship—really, one of the most critical aspects of friendship—is making sure that when there's a problem, you take care of it with the person who's involved and not take it first to the people around you. Someone once said, "A good friend won't stab you in the back. He'll stab you in the front." Yet it doesn't even need to be that weaponized; nobody needs to get stabbed. Earning the trust to enter the tunnel of chaos together is essential to getting through it. Your friend has to know that if there's a problem, you'll always come to him or her first.

It's an example of iron sharpening iron, a concept from the Bible. Proverbs 27:17 says, "As iron sharpens iron, so a friend sharpens a friend." It's not going into the conversation trying to convince the other person you're right. It's more about entering into it with a kind of curiosity, an attitude of exploration, keeping a vulnerable heart, and being willing to hear hard things and say hard things, if necessary. Once again, you're seeking clarity, not chaos. Sometimes the chaos comes anyway, but by embracing the "yes, and" while working through it together, you will emerge from the other side of the tunnel in a stronger, deeper relationship.

Eddie: There was the time when I got all up in your grill about where we were scheduled.

Tommy: Right. You were examining our schedule placement at several gigs, feeling like it wasn't the best fit for us.

Eddie: As we did more gigs, I was beginning to see a pattern of what worked for us and what didn't. And sometimes we'd make scheduling arrangements ahead of time, but then we'd get there and it'd be different. It was driving me crazy. So I'd come up to you and go, "Have you seen where they put us?"

Tommy: "Yeah."

Eddie: "Doesn't that make you mad?"

Tommy: "I have no feelings about it whatsoever."

Eddie: I'm trying to include you in my anger about it. And finally you said, "Hey, buddy, I'm not mad about it."

Tommy: And you're like, "Yes, you are."

Eddie: One day, you looked right at me and said, "Buddy, I don't get mad about stuff like this," and I'm aghast. I said, "Well, you should!" But that was the tunnel of chaos where I thought, *Wow, I really am controlling.*

Tommy: But the flip side of that is, I'm hearing that my opinion counts. That's what came out of that process for me. Used to be you'd ask, and I'd say, "I don't care," and you'd press into me with it. "Well, you gotta care."

Eddie: Your opinion counts.

Tommy: My opinion counts. And sometimes to this day, I still don't know what my opinion is, but I'm aware of it.

Eddie: And now there's comfort knowing you'll tell me your opinion.

Tommy: But then there was another tunnel of chaos, because as much as you wanted my opinion, when I started sharing my opinion, you had to get used to it. I told you at one point, "You can't ask me to share my opinion and then not want to hear it."

Eddie: I'd be like, "Well, you're sharing it wrong." But I think we've learned with each other over the years to say what we feel. We have that freedom, no matter how we feel.

Tommy: Like when you'd take food from places.

Eddie: Totally. We'd do a show, and they'd have all this food left over and want to send it with us. We knew we weren't going to eat it, but I'd walk out of there with this armful of food containers.

Tommy: And we're totally not going to eat it.

Eddie: Right. But I'm people-pleasing and not wanting to disappoint anyone. You finally said to me, "Why are you taking that food?" And I confessed that I didn't want to hurt their feelings.

Tommy: Saying no isn't going to hurt their feelings.

Eddie: It sounded so rude in my head! But you helped me see that I can just say, "No, we don't need the food."

Tommy: We already had our eye on two pizzas and a cheesecake.

Confronting a friend—whether it's something you feel they need to hear or expressing your true thoughts and feelings on a matter—takes courage, kindness, and a good measure of self-control. To do it well requires carefully examining your own motives going into it, as well as an offering of grace for the friend you're asking to walk the tunnel with you. But the more "tunnel of chaos" becomes part of your vocabulary, the more it also becomes part of the fabric of your friendship.

Even in our own ministry, we use the term and practice the tunnel of chaos with our staff. As you can imagine, the staff at Skit Guys is a creative and soulful bunch of people, which serves our ministry needs in terrific ways but can also work against us if we're not managing all of our relationships well. It's easy to just let the train roll on and expect it to arrive at its destination without a conductor. However, it's rarely the case that relationships are simply self-sustaining; they need attention, even in a work environment.

In our ministry, we do regular checkups to take the temperature of our staff and our friendships. We allow ourselves to go through the tunnel of chaos, even if it takes half the afternoon. And yes, we will sometimes pick up the phone and say, "Hey, I need to go through the tunnel of chaos with you." We teach the principle to our staff because not everyone was raised in an environment where expressing emotions was okay. Many people have never entered the tunnel of chaos with another person, let alone walked all the way through it and out the other side.

It's really a very cherished part of our ministry. You might think it would scare people off, but instead it shows our staff that we're in it with them for the long haul, that we're willing to make the emotional investment of listening and trying to understand.

Because the two of us have practiced it together, we're better able to implement it in our other relationships.

WHEN THE TUNNEL OF CHAOS GOES OFF THE RAILS

As you can imagine, the tunnel of chaos can derail in all sorts of ways. As much as we'd like to believe we can ride that goose from one end to the other in calm waters, we know that sometimes it doesn't work that way. Sometimes we end up wandering in the dark, trying to find the end of the tunnel, and wondering why we entered it in the first place.

Tommy: We should mention that we don't do the tunnel of chaos when prescription steroids are involved. That is a primary Tunnel of Chaos Rule. If a doctor prescribes you steroids, the tunnel is closed for "repairs."

Eddie: Yeah, I'm not myself on steroids.

Tommy: That's an understatement, Bruce Banner.

Eddie: And you know, the whole time I'm thinking, *No, I'm good. I'm fine. I'm very aware. I'm totally under control.*

Tommy: We tried "The sun's getting low, big guy," but it didn't work. The roof of my Jeep still has my fist marks in it from the time we went through the tunnel of chaos when you were 'roiding up and I was driving to Dallas.

Eddie: The silverback came out. And it is never good when the silverback is fighting the Incredible Hulk.

Tommy: But there are times when steroids aren't involved, and we're really just trying to relate, trying to get some things out, and it goes south. Like the time I wrongly interpreted your offering of grace.

Eddie: Oh, yeah!

Tommy: As per usual, you were working on bettering yourself while I was content being content with myself. You were reading some book about grace.

Eddie: *Grace-Based Parenting.*

Tommy: That was it.

Eddie: And I'd had this sort of epiphany as I was raising my two little girls that I might be passing on to them some things involving my control issues I didn't want to pass on. I knew I wasn't a very graceful person, so for me to learn grace, I started saying this phrase: "Hey, there's grace. There's grace."

Tommy: And I was starting to realize how I was dropping the ball on some things, and so I apologized to you for it. And you'd say to me, "Hey man, there's grace." You were saying that to me all the time.

Eddie: Yeah, in my head I was like, *Show grace. Show grace.*

Tommy: But I was hearing, "Good gosh, you take a lot of grace. You have no idea what it's like to be your friend, but it takes a lot of grace. And in case you didn't hear it, I'm going to say it again."

Eddie: I was saying it all the time.

Tommy: Finally, I lost it and yelled, "When you say there's grace, you're really meaning there's no grace!"

Eddie: I was totally confused about what was going on. It was the "you don't hug me" moment all over again.

Tommy: I had your motivations completely wrong, so we had to walk through that long tunnel. But what's beautiful is that it made me realize you're a verbal processor. When you're saying, "Hey man, there's grace," you're teaching yourself. It doesn't have anything to do with me.

Eddie: It took us both a while to unpack what was going on there.

Tommy: We've learned a lot in the tunnel of chaos, though none of our walks through them are ever the same. Except we've now politely asked your wife, Steph, to let us know when you're on steroids. As a courtesy.

Eddie: Completely understandable. There is no level of self-awareness that can prevent 'roid rage.

HOW TO KNOW YOUR FRIEND IS ON PRESCRIPTION STEROIDS

1. You go to Taco Bueno, and your friend orders the Wholotta Box of twelve tacos. Then he or she says, "What are you having?"

2. There are teeth marks on the stress ball you gave your friend for Christmas.

3. You're driving somewhere together, and you hear a low growl coming from the passenger seat.

4. You realize you've never noticed that vein pattern in your friend's neck before.

5. Your friend can now lift a small Kia.

TUNNEL OF CHAOS RULES

Once you've chosen to enter the tunnel of chaos, you may encounter sudden emotional turns and detours that throw the conversation off the track you intended. Another person's reaction is unpredictable, and no matter how well you prepare, you can't know what's going to happen until it happens.

However, following a few basic rules can help defuse tension and act as a good flashlight in the dark.

Try to Stay in the Room

As long as your temper is in check, try to keep the conversation going. Our natural instinct is to flee when conflict arises, but being willing to participate in the "and" part of "yes, and" will actually be a comfort to the other person. It signals that you're in this for the long haul, that you're not just trying to criticize a behavior or air a hurt, but rather, your motivation is the good of the relationship. In short, you're there because you care.

Keep Your Voice Down

IT'S NATURAL TO WANT TO BE HEARD. AND EVEN IF YOU'RE NOT ANGRY, IT'S EASY TO TURN UP THE VOLUME TO TRY TO MAKE SURE YOUR POINT IS HEARD. BUT AS YOU CAN SEE, IT'S REALLY ANNOYING. NOT ONLY THAT, BUT LOUD THINGS OFTEN SIGNAL "DANGER!" PLUS, IT CAN BE DISCONCERTING FOR THE OTHER PERSON TO TALK OVER ALL THAT NOISE.

Therefore, keep your volume at a steady, moderate level so you're not adding an uncomfortable distraction.

Side note on anger: it's a God-given emotion, but we can abuse it. Anger can be just as addictive as a drug. We should seldom get angry, yet a lot of us live on the verge of anger; it's our go-to emotion. Anger tells us we need to take action, and all too often that action is "writing the end of the chapter" of a situation or relationship. If you find yourself angry all the time, friendships will soon crumble. So before you sit in the goose and go through the tunnel, work on the anger issues.

3 Be Willing to Listen

For many of us, it's in our nature to want to fix other people, so when there's a problem, we assume it's the other person who needs to make the adjustment. We humans can often be impervious to our own blind spots. Real progress in a friendship comes by expressing the problem and then listening to the other person's perspective, even before offering your own. Keep an open mind going in, and shine the spotlight on the problem without being so quick to offer your own solution.

4 Respond Instead of React

James 1:19 (MSG) says, "Post this at all the intersections, dear friends: Lead with your ears, follow up with your tongue, and let anger straggle along in the rear." What a beautiful reminder of how to walk through the tunnel! Reacting only makes the tunnel longer. Responding, however, makes for a safe environment for both parties to travel together. Sometimes the difference between reacting and responding may be subtle, but the impact is huge.

Try not to get defensive and take things personally. Listen and seek to understand. Stick with phrases like "I feel . . ." instead of "Well, you . . ." And try not to interrupt. If you're interrupting, you really aren't hearing or listening; you just want to fight.

Reaction leads with accusations and emotion. Responding listens and confirms that what the other person has said is being heard and processed.

5 Prepare for a Long Tunnel

Some tunnels are short. Others are long. Remember to keep your eye on the long game, the ultimate purpose of the talk. The point of entering the tunnel is not to win or be right. If that's your headspace, the goose wins. Rather, it's to invest in the relationship. The relationship is the thing that drives you to walk in. Every time.

And remember, you don't leave your friend in the tunnel. You may walk out with things unresolved at this time, but you don't walk out alone.

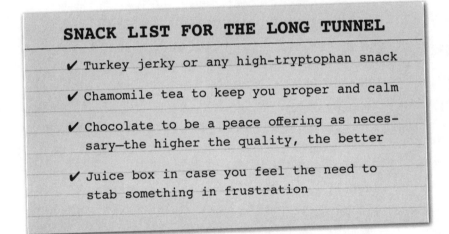

SNACK LIST FOR THE LONG TUNNEL

✔ Turkey jerky or any high-tryptophan snack

✔ Chamomile tea to keep you proper and calm

✔ Chocolate to be a peace offering as necessary—the higher the quality, the better

✔ Juice box in case you feel the need to stab something in frustration

THE LIGHT AT THE END OF THE TUNNEL

To conclude, the more relationships you form, the more tunnels you'll encounter—but the less scary they'll be. And you will find yourself leading some friends into it who have never been in one, never "floated the goose." Be patient with them. Start small and work your way up to bigger issues. Make your newbie feel secure in the relationship. Help them understand that you're not going anywhere, that you're invested—in them.

To hear from someone that no matter what tunnel you're in, you're not coming out without them . . . well, that's the kind of friendship people are drawn to. That kind of friendship is very rare.

When you're willing to work in the dirt, come springtime, you won't believe what will bloom.

Tommy: Also remember that not everything requires going into the tunnel of chaos. Sometimes, you just let your friend believe that the bird is a goose even when you're 100 percent sure it's a swan.

Eddie: What?! That is just not true.

Tommy: Buddy, the swan is the international bird of love. The goose is something people eat in a Charles Dickens novel.

Eddie: You waited till the end of the chapter to bring this up?

Tommy: As I said, not everything requires going into the tunnel.

Eddie: Please buckle up and keep your hands and feet inside the swan—I mean, goose—for the entire ride.

Tommy: Okay, but we're getting a funnel cake when we're done.

Think of a time you entered the tunnel of chaos with someone and it didn't go well. Analyze how it could have gone differently. Think about your actions and how you would change them in light of what you learned in this chapter. Pray about talking to that person again and revisiting the issue with a new perspective

CHAPTER 6

My House Smells Like Bacon

A s we've said, if you want a good friend, you need to be a good friend. So what friendship traits should you be looking to develop to become a good friend? What are some things you can do to become the kind of friend someone looks at and says, "I want that person to be in my circle"?

If you think about it, the reason any of us want someone to be in our circle is mostly because of the person's character. Sure, there are other trappings that may draw us to like someone at first—personality, looks, status, stuff in common, money, and so on. But what we're talking about now is a whole other level. To allow someone into our Garden Circle, we must look at someone's life and want something they have inside. We're talking about character, values, some intentionality to how they go about living their life. Character is defined as a group of qualities, such as integrity, honesty, empathy, and compassion, that makes a person unique, makes them stand out. Character isn't easy to come by, and when we see it, we want to know how that person came to be the person they are.

How do we ourselves become people of good character? This always involves taking steps to move out of our comfort zone and begin helping others. This is what it means to "let your light shine before others, that they may see your good deeds and glorify your Father in heaven" (Matthew 5:16, NIV).

Eddie: Speaking of good deeds, do you remember when I lived with you and Angie for a while?

Tommy: Remember? I think of it every time I see, smell, or taste bacon.

Eddie: I love bacon.

Tommy: Oh, I know.

Eddie: I was moving back from California, I wasn't married, and I didn't have a place to stay. You were newly married and opened your home to me and said I could stay with you.

Tommy: Newly-ish. We'd been married five years, I think. You were hardcore on the Atkins diet, so you were cooking bacon all the time—like, every morning. I was working at a church, and I would come home at night and wonder, *Why does the house smell like bacon?*

Eddie: Bacon and Polish sausage. I had no idea. I'm just obliviously cooking bacon. Grease is everywhere. I tried to clean it up, but, you know—

Tommy: We lived in a church parsonage. So it already smelled like old preachers. Angie had this aging cat named Lester, who had an incontinence problem. Then you show up and add bacon to the old-preacher/cat-pee smell. In hindsight, your bacon probably improved the overall smell of the house.

Eddie: They make candles out of those kinds of smells nowadays, so you're welcome.

Tommy: That's not really what I was trying to say.

Eddie: I said you're welcome. No need to thank me.

Tommy: I wasn't going to.

Eddie: Ungrateful . . .

Tommy: I think the point of the story is that I did something nice for YOU!

Eddie: Oh. Okay, I see it now. Yep. Apologies. And thank you.

The good deeds of a friendship include carefully studying what those could and should be and how they could benefit your friend. It's easy to be on the receiving end of a good deed but forget to be a giver of them. It's also easy to get comfortable in a relationship, take it for granted, and forget to look for what you might be able to give.

Even the simplest gestures of acknowledgment toward a friend make a huge impact. And when those gestures continue, year after year, you've got something really special going—

Eddie: Again, sorry, talking a lot here—

Tommy: We are the authors, so . . .

Eddie: The first years of our adult friendship were really a test of this principle.

Tommy: There was an entirely new dynamic. It was no longer "just us buddies" doing our thing. I was working for this church and trying to also do skits with you, and I now had a wife I was supporting. And when I say "supporting," I mean she was supporting us financially. I was making a youth pastor salary at a small church—$16,000 a year. But they did let me live in the old-preacher/cat-pee-smelling house.

Eddie: Right, and I laugh thinking back on it now, but you would come in from an exhausting day of work—

Tommy: Totally whipped. The thing about working at a church is that although you don't make much money, you work all the time. I remember coming in one day, a Wednesday night around nine o'clock, and I'm exhausted and hungry.

Eddie: And I'm in your recliner, I think.

Tommy: Yeah, with my favorite blanket. The house still smells like bacon, of course. Angie's on the couch under a blanket, all comfortable. Outside there's ten inches of snow and bone-chilling cold, and I drove uphill both ways. The tag is itchy on my shirt . . . You get the idea. Did I mention I'm also hungry?

Eddie: And Angie and I are watching *Waiting to Exhale*. Whitney Houston. I guess chick flicks were always a running theme with us . . .

Tommy: I'm standing there thinking, *Nobody even cares I'm home. They've got their jambalaya and their "shoop, shoop" movie.* But my mood shifts when I realize Angie has cooked one of her famous Louisiana meals, homemade jambalaya. My favorite.

Eddie: But because I was doing Atkins, I had gone through and picked out all the meat. Angie, bless her heart, just let that pass.

Tommy: I go to dish up a bowl of jambalaya, and there is maybe one piece of sausage left in there. Basically, I'm left with a bowl of rice for dinner, and I am TICKED.

Eddie: Oh, buddy . . . yeah, that was a rough moment. But we talked through it all. I mean, you were stretched pretty thin.

Tommy: Yeah, I was trying to do too much. Our church didn't have a senior pastor, and our worship pastor had left. So I was running the youth ministry, leading worship, and preaching in three services. And on top of that, you and I had started traveling and doing skits.

Eddie: And at one point during my stay, Angie comes to my room, and she's so upset, and she's like, "Eddie, I found Tommy in the fetal position in the bathroom, and I don't know what to do. This isn't like him."

Tommy: It was really a great moment in our friendship. She was scared, and you got to be a calm voice in a rough storm.

Eddie: It felt good to give back since I was basically a squatter. I just sat with you on that bathroom floor and consoled you. For the first time in our adult lives, the tables had turned a bit. The buddy who invited me to church and taught me how to tithe was looking to me for comfort. That's friendship. It takes courage on both parts. Could I step up to the plate and be what he needed me to be? And could Superman take off his cape long enough to say he doesn't have it all together? Nothing else mattered in that bacon-ridden, cat-infested parsonage.

Tommy: It is a beautiful thing, the way friendship works. I didn't open my home to you out of obligation. Someone I loved was in need. It wasn't a question of if we would take you in; that's what friends do. At the same time, God was bringing you into our home to help me through a difficult time. You joined me on the front lines by living with us.

Eddie: And by the way, I totally changed over to turkey bacon too. Less splatter-y, and it didn't stink up the whole house.

Tommy: So kind of you.

Strengthening Already-Strong Bonds

The story of the bacon and of our learning to shift the dynamics of our friendship shows the effort it takes to make things work. Here are a few practices that can strengthen the existing strong bonds within a friendship. These may seem obvious, but it's rare for friends to give them a lot of thought before tensions or crises arise.

GIFT FROM EDDIE TO TOMMY

1 Evaluating the Give and Take

When we're younger, it hardly occurs to us what we're taking in any relationship. Friendships tend to be a little easier when we're young because, frankly, we're not thinking a whole lot about balance. But as we grow and mature, physically and spiritually, we begin to see the world differently. As we spend more time in the Word of God and allow it to saturate us, our perspective eventually flips to where we're prepared to give more than we take. Applying an attitude of servanthood to our friendships will only strengthen them.

Eddie: You know, when we're on the road, people really receive the fact that our friendship comes before ministry.

Tommy: Yes, when we talk about this at gigs, it always gets applause, doesn't it?

Eddie: I think people can appreciate that our friendship comes first.

Tommy: If what we do—our gigs, our tours— begins to threaten our friendship, then we know we have to deal with it. Because something is out of whack.

Eddie: Those are the iron-sharpens-iron moments. We have dealt with some things over the years, trying to make sure we keep everything in its place.

Tommy: We should talk about that.

Eddie: We should. First, let me get a snack. Why am I craving bacon? Do I have time to make some bacon?

Tommy: But we're right in the middle . . . there he goes. Okay. Stand by. His blood sugar gets low, and he gets hangry. We're better off if we let him grab a snack. Plus, he always brings back some for me.

2 Inviting In and Letting Go

Maybe it's a strange juxtaposition, this idea of "inviting in and letting go." It's opening the door to your whole life—your home, your soul, your fears, your victories—while also keeping the door open should the other person ever feel the need to walk out.

The fragile thing about friendship is that you can't rely on your friends for happiness. They bring happiness, but they're not your happiness. The instant you put your life's happiness in another's hands, then you've become codependent, meaning you are dependent on someone else to give your life worth. To do so is to put pressure on them they'll be unable to handle and never be able to carry. A friend is a supplement to your life, an addition, not the whole focus of it. A friend must know that if they need to go, for whatever reason, you won't stop them—and you'll bless them on the way out.

3 Consider Their Family and Yours

Sometimes we feel the urge to place a friendship in a neat, tidy, safe box.

This is my "pool hall buddy."

This is my "Thursday night basketball friend."

This is my "girls' night out pal."

That's fine and well for friends in your Hang-Out and Acquaintance circles and, to a limited extent, your Circle of Honor. But a next-level Garden friendship brings in your spouse, your kids, your hurts, your dreams, your pain, your celebrations—the whole enchilada. Garden-level friendship is a big ol' welcome mat to your life.

So know that if you go into a friendship wishing your friend's spouse would get out of the way of all the fun, you're in for a disaster. Once a spouse is involved, he or she is part of the equation and will always be part of the equation. Making sure everyone is on board with this will go a long way toward maintaining marital bliss. The Beatles as a group were disintegrating long before John Lennon's new wife, Yoko Ono, got involved. Still, to this day, her name is used to describe a squashed friendship or enterprise: "Yeah, we were fine until his wife Yoko'd the whole situation."

It can be tricky to make the transition if the friendship was formed before the spouse was in the picture. But allowing the spouse to be a central part of the relationship—and making sure the spouse doesn't feel threatened by the friendship—will only enhance it.

Mixing a spouse into the friendship certainly complicates the dynamic. Introducing two spouses to the mixture is exponentially more complicated, given the many intricacies, insecurities, and history involved. It's almost like dating a new person. Will the spouses like one another? Even if they may never be as tight as the two friends, the hope is they'll develop a deep respect for each other. And if the original friendship produces good fruit, ideally the spouses will be able to see that the relationship brings out the best in their mates, which in turn strengthens both marriages.

On the other hand, it's a telltale sign if one of the marriages is suffering because of the friendship. That's a sure indication that the friendship needs close examination and change.

Be patient when introducing a spouse to a close friend or vice versa. It takes time. It takes respect. It takes effort for anyone to learn about a whole new personality. Be willing to be a second or third or fourth wheel in your friend's life. It's part of the sacrifice, part of the gift that you're willing to give to keep that person in your life.

When your friend's spouse sees that you're not a threat, the usual response will be to open the door and let you in.

And if you're on the other side, feeling threatened by your spouse's friendships, reconsider your feelings. If the friendship seems otherwise healthy, it can be a wonderful enhancement to your spouse's life and to yours. Open your door and put out the mat.

Building friendships with families in mind can be a real blessing if you let it.

Bottom line: Good friendships can be good for marriages.

It just takes consideration—on all sides.

Tommy: You're back.

Eddie: I am. Care for a ninety-calorie mixed nut snack pack? It has pistachios. We had no bacon.

Tommy: Told you he'd bring me some.

Eddie: So as I was saying—

Tommy: I've completely lost track.

Eddie: Well, what I wanted to say is that our wives play a huge part in our ministry.

Tommy: For sure.

Eddie: You hear about bands and ministries breaking up because a wife or husband is going, "I can't take you being gone all the time." And then it's over. I mean, have you ever had a moment with Angie where it's like, "I don't know about the Skit Guys thing"?

Tommy: No. She supports me wholeheartedly. But maybe we could've used a few moments of our wives reining us back in some. I know I've missed out on some things that would have been great not to miss out on. But that's not my family's fault.

Eddie: It could've been a totally different dynamic, with our wives standing outside the circle, looking in, not really being a part of it all. But it's not like that. There was always a welcome mat there.

Tommy: I mean, we've had to work through a few things. Like sometimes Angie would be disappointed when I went to a movie with you while we were traveling because she wanted to go see that movie with me.

Eddie: And I could get sort of upset we'd end up going to some stupid movie I didn't want to see. So there have been pushes and pulls.

Tommy: But you eventually worked to a point where you'll say, "Hey, do you want to go see this movie, or is that something you and Angie want to go see?" It's taking into consideration the other part of me, my spouse.

Eddie: And Steph doesn't go see movies, so either I see them with you or I go alone, but that's part of the equation. If Angie wants the experience of seeing a particular movie for the first time with you, I want to respect that.

Tommy: Even though I'm happy to see it again. I'll go see movies twice.

Eddie: But I'm not just friends with you. I'm friends with Angie, too.

Tommy: And our kids. We've taken on the mantle of being uncle to each other's kids. Being there for them. Encouraging them.

Eddie: And there have been times when we have each taken up the side of the other's wife—

Tommy: Which I'm sure at the time we didn't take well.

Eddie: True, but we never tear down the other's wife. We don't go there.

Tommy: We never go there.

#PROTIP

Things not to say to your best friend's spouse:

X "I'll probably be leaving your house around 3 a.m. or so."

X "I'm so sorry I spilled that. Can you clean it up?"

X "I hear you had a fight. Can I give you my opinion on the matter?"

X "Surprise! I'm going on vacation with you!"

X "Are you still here?"

---

4 ## Sacrificing Your Time and Effort

In this day and age of cocooning, it's easy to get comfortable within the walls of our homes. So when the doorbell rings, we slide out of our recliners and belly crawl across the carpet like a Marine so as not to be detected by the person at the door. Or the awkward moment when you're texting with someone, and they decide to call you—there's no sending the caller to voicemail. They know you're available.

It's easier to lock the doors, pull the shutters, and watch five hours of Netflix than to engage with the outside world, with real people. But "easy" doesn't get you Garden friends. "Easy" gets you Acquaintances and maybe Hang-Out friends. One day, you may look back on your life and realize your only friends are fictional characters on TV.

If you're longing for better, deeper relationships, be willing to do things that are uncomfortable or inconvenient. Know a friend is moving? Ask if you can help. Heard their fence blew down? Bring some tools and pitch in to hammer up a few slats. Learn a friend is sick with whatever's going around? Pick up their favorite coffee and leave it on their doorstep. Make the investment.

Remember that real investment will always be inconvenient. Some people are created with personalities that compel them to never stop doing things for others. The rest of us, not so much. Perhaps it takes work to leave your house and go serve someone else. But making an investment in the life of someone you think is worthy of championing will likely pay off in great ways down the road.

Mind you, the results may not be immediate. We're so used to living in a fast-food, on-demand, TikTok culture, and we want our instant gratification now. But you will find over time, as you and your friend do life together, the personal rewards get better and better. Rich relationships are cultivated and nurtured and grown in soil where both people are vulnerable and committed.

In the movie *A League of Their Own*, the Tom Hanks character, Jimmy the manager, confronts Dottie, played by Geena Davis, when she wants to quit baseball and go home to the farm.

"It just got too hard," Dottie says.

Jimmy responds, "It's supposed to be hard. If it wasn't hard, everyone would do it. The hard is what makes it great."

That's true in friendships, too. The hard is what makes it great. After all, it's easy to gather up superficial relationships. But when you find a person with good character worthy of being emulated, someone who will always build you up rather than tear you down, then even when life gets messy, you do the work. That's the hard. That's the investment.

5 Celebrating Successes

Oscar Wilde, or someone who sounds like him on the internet, said, "Anybody can sympathize with the sufferings of a friend, but it requires a very fine nature to sympathize with a friend's success."

Opening up your life, or walking into the open door of someone else's, requires not just keeping watch in their pain and suffering, weeping with them when they mourn, but also rejoicing with them in their best successes (Romans 12:15).

How do you feel when your friend gets an enormous raise?

How do you feel when a friend gets married before you?

How do you feel when a friend leaves for their dream vacation?

You can measure very quickly the health of the friendship—not to mention your own soul—by how you react to a friend's good news. Pause and ask yourself, *Do I celebrate friends' successes when they share good news?* Or are you more apt to cut them down a bit, dissing their talent or hard work by pointing out an unrelated reason as to why this good thing probably happened? What feelings are you process-ing—for example, jealousy, envy, or anger—that good things always seem to happen to everyone else but you?

Celebration is too rare a thing in families and in friendships. If you make an effort to look for things, big and small, to celebrate in the lives of others, your friends will thank you for it. Deeper relationships in life require walking through all the doors. And keeping jealousy in check can be one of the harder challenges at times. But it's also a tool by which your character will be sharpened by God—if you'll let Him use it.

Eddie: Aflac.

Tommy: What are you doing?

Eddie: Whatever do you mean? Quack, quack.

Tommy: Oh! I get it. So here's the thing Daffy is cuing me to bring up. I was visiting family in Louisiana with Angie. And our friend Mac—

Eddie: Quack.

Tommy: —invited me to go meet the *Duck Dynasty* folks.

Eddie: And not me. [lets out a terribly sad quack]

Tommy: So we spent the day at Phil Robertson and Miss Kay's house. They made us lunch and showed us around their land. If you follow me on Instagram, you saw the pictures. It was pretty cool.

Eddie: And a little piece of my soul died.

Tommy: Yes, in hindsight, I could have asked if they would mind if my friend and his family joined us. I just didn't want to impose. You know how I am.

Eddie: And honestly, I could have celebrated you getting to do something cool even if it was without me.

Tommy: I get it. Celebrating someone else's good fortune is like watching your friend play a video game—the only thought going through your head is, *When do I get to play?*

Eddie: It's those moments, though, when we get to feel the feelings but decide how to respond. I had to work through it and arrive at the thought, *I'm a little jealous, but they didn't do it on purpose. It wasn't personal.* From there it became, *I'm happy for them.* That's super cool they got to do that together. It took me a few steps to get to celebration mode, but in the end, I'd much rather get there than just stew in my own misery. And when I can celebrate someone else's success and truly mean it without a "why" on my end—well, that's the guy I want to be.

Tommy: Don't beat yourself up. Who gave me forty gifts for my fortieth birthday? Talk about celebrating!

Eddie: I think, for the most part, we've tried to celebrate each other and our families. You gave me Sid Caesar's jacket that Eddie Murphy gave him when he guest-hosted *SNL* in 1983. You bought that for my birthday! Sid Caesar's honorary cast jacket! Who does that?! You've driven three hours to watch my kids perform in their school plays, and I've driven the same to watch your kids perform in their plays. We want our families to feel the extension of love and know that their lives are worth celebrating.

Tommy: We try to celebrate the little things because, in the end, they are big.

We've come a long way since those days at the parsonage . . .

Eddie: I wonder if that house still smells like bacon.

Tommy: The church tore it down after we moved out.

Eddie: For real?

Tommy: Yeah. Seems the smell of old pastor, cat pee, and bacon was a sign from God.

Eddie: I think I remember that being a sign of the end times in Revelation.

Tommy: Speaking of end times, should we end the chapter or . . . ?

FABLE OF THE CHICKEN AND THE PIG

Once upon a time there was a beloved breakfast called bacon and eggs. Everyone loved bacon and eggs, but few understood the lessons to be learned from the glorious breakfast pairing. You see, the chicken provides the eggs. And the pig provides the bacon. The chicken is committed to the dish, but for the pig, it requires his sacrifice. **#bethebacon**

EDDIE'S FAMOUS BACON RECIPE

1. Start with a cold pan.

2. Put as much bacon in the pan as you can without overcrowding.

3. Turn the heat to medium high.

4. As the bacon cooks, use a portable fan to send the smell wafting through the house.

5. When the bacon grease splatters, use your fingers to wipe it up, and then lick your fingers.

6. As the bacon starts to crisp, flip it.

7. After it crisps more, take the individual pieces out of the pan and place them on paper towels to drain. Or straight into your mouth. Whatever.

8. Eat all the pieces before anyone else comes into the kitchen.*

9. Use the paper towels as future handkerchiefs.

Step 8 is not recommended for anyone hoping to stay off cholesterol medication.

CHAPTER 7

ONUS ON ME

HAIKU POETRY:
A "BLAME-SHIFTING" DUEL

I see you're upset—

to find the one you can blame

look in the mirror

by Eddie James

Why are you so mad?

You want me to say "my bad"—

your approach is sad

by Tommy Woodard

You have no regrets?

I don't mean to throw such shade;

mistakes have been made

by Eddie James

Tommy: We are really terrible at this.

Eddie: We should just fight the old-fashioned way.

WHO'S SORRY NOW?

In his biography of Abraham Lincoln, the poet Francis Fisher Browne told the story of Charles Scott, a colonel in the U.S. Army who was assigned to guard the Capitol during the Civil War. Scott's wife had died tragically, and he'd written his superiors to ask for time off to attend his wife's funeral and be with his children. However, all the way up the chain of command, his request was denied. Furious, Colonel Scott made an appeal directly to President Lincoln, believing him to be a compassionate man. However, Scott's appeal was met with a scathing rejection during an audience with the exhausted president, who told the grieving soldier he couldn't be bothered and to let the War Department handle it. "If they cannot help you," Lincoln said, "then bear your burden, as we all must, until the war is over."

Colonel Scott was understandably crushed. But to his surprise, the next morning, the president stood at his door, offering an apology: "I have no excuse for my conduct. Indeed, I was weary to the last extent; but I had no right to treat a man with rudeness who had offered his life for his country, much more a man who came to me in great affliction. I have had a regretful night, and come now to beg your forgiveness."

Nothing can strengthen a friendship like the ability to apologize. Just as important, nothing can weaken one faster than an inability to say the words "I'm sorry." Yet an apology is one of the hardest things to navigate in life and in friendship.

Let's start with the definition of an apology—the really easy definition. It's admitting you were wrong and expressing regret for your actions or words.

Knowing you need to apologize requires self-awareness. It also takes the effort of self-evaluation, which many of us don't or won't take the time to do. A good apology takes prayer and thoughtfulness and a hefty amount of pride-swallowing. But working your way through this process in a healthy manner is the tilling of the soil required for any relationship to develop good, strong roots.

Eddie: I am so, so sorry, but we have to cut in for a second and explain ourselves.

Tommy: The truth is, we could've written an entire book on apology disasters.

Eddie: To be honest, I was the people-pleaser who wanted to be liked by everyone. And if I felt like I let someone down, even strangers . . . well, let's just say I had a habit of apologizing for everything.

Tommy: Meanwhile, I was completely oblivious to my own offenses.

Eddie: I carried a ton of resentment because I thought, Tommy doesn't understand. He doesn't care. That's how I interpreted it. But we knew we had to get a hold of it because as the ministry grew, we weren't just buddies anymore; we were in business together. So this led to a lot more tunnel-of-chaos moments.

Tommy: There was so much self-righteousness in me that I didn't think I needed to apologize. I always thought I was right and that you were the one who should apologize. So you had to figure out not everything was your fault, and I had to figure out some things were, in fact, my fault.

Eddie: But then we both read a book on apologies.

Tommy: And one of the most important things we learned from that book is that—

Eddie: Wait a second.

Tommy: What?

Eddie: We should wait to tell them.

Tommy: Why?

Eddie: It's called a cliffhanger.

Tommy: I don't know if that qualifies.

Eddie: Sure it does. That's the kind of thing that makes for a page-turner. Readers will be on the edge of their seats, going, "I have to know! I have to!"

Tommy: I don't think anyone is saying that. Instead, we should tell the story about when you were hanging off that cliff at Pigeon Forge.

Eddie: That didn't happen.

Tommy: I know. I'm just trying to show you what a cliffhanger is.

Eddie: What if instead you think of a great story about when you apologized to me?

Tommy: Or how we got through your tardiness problem.

Eddie: Okay, look. Let's at least explore the five types of dysfunctional apologies.

Tommy: That sounds as fun as a stomach virus.

Eddie: A necessary purging of the toxins in our life, my friend.

Tommy: I'll get the air freshener.

FIVE TYPES OF APOLOGIES THAT BOMB

We'd love to say that in our friendship of thirty-five-plus years, we've nailed the fine art of apologizing. But in fact, we could truly write the book on how not to do it. We've been guilty of totally butchering apologies. Maybe you have too. And you've probably been on the receiving end of an apology that falls flat. The word *sorry* is in there, but nothing is made right, and you feel an emptiness inside of you—a hollow reaction to a hollow word. Let's look at five types of apologies that never get off the ground.

"I'm sorry, but . . ."

An apology that attaches a qualifier to it isn't an apology at all. You're saying the words, but you're placing blame elsewhere. When you put a condition on your apology, you fail to take ownership of your part of the wrong. This is actually an excuse disguised as an apology.

"I'm sorry that hurt you."

Notice how the second "I" is missing here? This apology falls way short because although you're acknowledging that somebody's feelings have been hurt, you're putting the onus on them. It's as if you're saying, "I feel sorry you feel hurt, but I don't think that's my fault." Again, this is shifting blame to the person who was hurt. It's not taking any kind of ownership of your actions at all. You're making the offended person feel worse about themselves rather than working to mend the relationship.

The sentence should always be "I'm sorry that I hurt you." Yes, those are hard words to say without editing them as a form of self-defense. Being wrong is tough to own up to. Pride does some of its best work in these situations.

"I'm sorry
(that you're not sorry)."

Let's say you and a friend have had a fight, and there's this big, gaping opportunity for your friend to apologize. And you're sort of waiting for that apology to come, but it's not coming. So you decide this is a great time for a teaching moment: I'll say I'm sorry so she'll say she's sorry. That'll work! So you say you're sorry, probably not really meaning it because it's actually an opening for your friend to say she's sorry.

Crickets.

No apology comes. And now you're fuming twice as hard because you swallowed your pride, said you're sorry, and you're getting nothing in return. Double offense!

Trying to bait an apology always fails because it starts with a false motive. This is just a lie disguised as an apology, because let's be honest, you weren't really sorry when you said it.

"I'm sorry for everything."

If you suffer from codependency or people-pleasing, you know the urge. It sometimes feels uncontrollable, doesn't it? You just want peace. You hate conflict. You'll do anything, including apologize for the weather, if it makes everyone comfortable.

"I'm sorry, did you want to go first?"

"I'm sorry for picking this chair to sit in. Do you want it?"

"I'm sorry I didn't see you wave at me."

"I'm sorry I was in your way."

"I'm sorry . . ."

"I'm sorry . . ."

"I'm sorry . . ."

At first glance, it can seem polite. But for many, it's a way of life. It's what you say, but it also becomes what you believe about yourself. That you are less than. That problems are your fault. This mindset can be extremely damaging to you and also to those around you, because it lets friends and family off the hook. They never have to take responsibility for anything because you're taking it all.

 ## 5   "I'm sorry, okay?"

This apology is flippant and said with virtually no meaning or warmth in it. You're not apologizing; you're just trying to get past it. Perhaps you even recognize that you messed up, but you're unwilling to say it. Your pride won't let you. This terse apology never works, and it can inflict even more damage than staying silent.

Eddie: Is it our turn to speak?

Tommy: It's always our turn to speak.

Eddie: Okay! Reveal time! Tell them the thing that helped us turn the corner in our friendship.

Tommy: Totally. I'm still not sure it was a good fit for a cliffhanger, but anyway, we came to realize that an apology . . . it has to cost you something.

Eddie: Yes! Yes! Isn't that a great thing? You have to take ownership of it, not just point it out.

Tommy: There are no "ifs" or "buts." It's just saying, "That's on me. I'm taking ownership."

Eddie: And we say that to each other: "Onus on me." We have learned to take responsibility.

Tommy: It really is an essential step in learning how to apologize. And once you learn it, it's amazing how it gets picked up by others.

THE COST OF AN APOLOGY

We have a mutual friend who tells the story of his father, who was by no means a perfect dad. But when his dad made a mistake, was wrong, or used poor judgment, he would always apologize. His dad took the onus for errors resulting from his own insecurities or bad judgments.

Our friend can smile now when he says,

My dad was the first to apologize and say he messed up. The older I got, the more I saw what a beautiful thing that was, saying he was wrong. That had to take guts and surely was embarrassing at times. Still, he did it. And that, in turn, took a ton of pressure off me growing up. When it was his fault, he owned it. And that's a great character trait for a father to have. That is life-changing.

There are two parts to an apology, two things that cost the person giving it. And if you're not willing to pay the price, there's no reason to offer the apology in the first place. Sorry is just a word without some sacrifice attached to it.

 # Taking Ownership

This is a hard thing to do. As we've mentioned, in our friendship and among our staff, we use the phrase "Onus on me." Onus is a noun used to refer to something that is one's duty or responsibility. It's a funny-sounding phrase, but it says all that needs to be said: "That's on me. I take responsibility for that." Sometimes we'll even pat our chest, to make sure it's understood.

Once you begin taking responsibility for things you do wrong, you begin to break down the wall of pride. Pride is one of the biggest barriers to transparency and security in any relationship. You can't always be looking out for number one.

You can also take ownership for something that you didn't know at the time was hurtful. If someone has been hurt and you don't understand it, take the time to figure it out. Ask, "What hurt you?" about this or that. Sit down and listen. Stop using all your energy to defend yourself.

If you will sit down with someone who is upset with you and say, "Help me understand," you will see their walls of defense and anger start to come down. It's kind of amazing to watch. And it's so rare that it can take people by surprise.

Taking ownership of a hurt you've caused is an invaluable gift you give to another person. It's saying with true conviction, "I care about you." And it can strengthen your friendship or relationship more than you ever expected. You'll find that it also does amazing work in your own heart, too.

Making Change

The second part of the sacrifice is the action part. You can be sorry and really mean it, but if you continue to inflict the same injury over and over without addressing the cause, your apologies are empty. Sometimes, this is where the tunnel of chaos begins. Some conflicts and issues need more than an apology; they need to be worked out. The two of you need to sit down, try to understand each other, and come to an agreement you can both live with.

A simplified formula for an apology might look something like this:

Empathy (considering their feelings)

\+ **Offense** (naming and owning what you did)

\+ **Apology** (saying "I'm sorry")

\+ **Change** (taking action to address the cause)

= **FORGIVENESS** (hopefully!)

Eddie: So, perfect example of this: I'm notorious for being late.

Tommy: True story.

Eddie: We've worked through it in some funny ways. I mean, you could've said, "Hey, this bothers me—you don't think my time is valuable" or whatever.

Tommy: Well, what actually happened is that one time I was late, and I was apologizing, and you said, "Hey, ten minutes is on time in my book."

Eddie: Ha! So I basically just justified it.

Tommy: And then there was this totally dysfunctional way I tried to handle your tardiness—I tried to prompt you to apologize by coming in the back door.

Eddie: What did you say?

Tommy: "Hey, I'm really sorry I'm such a stickler for being on time."

Eddie: Ha! I probably patted you on the shoulder and said, "That's okay. There's grace, buddy."

Tommy: Yeah, it backfired big-time. Made me even more mad.

Eddie: And then there was the unfortunate season when you decided to start being late too. So we showed up late together everywhere. But then you got a new job and suddenly started arriving on time everywhere, and I was just like, "Wait a minute. I thought we had a silent agreement to be late together!"

Tommy: Ha! Yeah, I remember that.

Eddie: But there was a whole season when you heard a lot of empty apologies from me. I felt like I meant them, but I was still late all the time.

Tommy: Then we learned to communicate.

Eddie: And I'm no longer chronically late. It's a thing I've worked on. If I'm late, I pick up the phone and say, "Hey, I need ten more minutes." And by the way, that story we told about our friend's dad has stayed with me. I try to do that with my girls, apologizing when I mess up. And it carries over into my marriage, too.

Tommy: Oh, me too. And with my dogs.

Eddie: Why do you apologize to your dogs?

Tommy: My wife buys them these organic peanut butter dog treats, and I'm telling you, it's like eating a Nutter Butter. Hard to stop at one.

Eddie: I feel like this might require you to change more than apologize.

Tommy: I'm working on it.

#PROTIP

In general, resist practicing apologies on dogs. These interactions may give you a false sense that the apology process is always going to be easy and will end with your face being licked.

THE MEASURE OF A FRIENDSHIP

As you're looking at your circles of friends and diving deeper into your relationships, pay careful attention to this aspect of friendship, the ability to apologize. It's a quick but effective measure of the health of your friendship.

If a friend you enjoy hanging with won't apologize to save his or her life, that's a red flag. Why? Because it leads to an imbalance in the friendship, throwing it off-kilter. At first, you might write off this tendency as a character quirk. But an inability to apologize sows seeds of bitterness, which in the long run will cause a lot of problems.

And by the way, apologizing is not a sign of weakness. It's really a sign of strength, to be able to acknowledge your imperfections and your mistakes. That's why it's essential not only to make it a practice in your own life but also look to develop relationships where it's practiced as well. When room is made for genuine apologies between two friends, this can lead to a deep connection that can't be replicated any other way.

When someone is willing to lay down their pride, drop all their walls, and tell you they are genuinely sorry, that's a friend to keep.

So if you begin to see a pattern where a person in your life can't apologize, be wary. You've talked to them, tried to reason with them, offered apologies yourself, and still the person won't apologize? The hard truth is that the friendship is probably not going anywhere. That person might remain an Acquaintance or Hang-Out friend, but they'll miss out on the opportunity to become a close friend. The truth is, some people just don't have it to give.

And the harder truth is that this can be true for all of us if we're not regularly feeding ourselves with the Word of God. When Jesus is involved, He gives us the ability to pour out beyond our own capabilities. His grace allows us—encourages us, even—to lay down our pride and take up His love instead. We don't have anything to defend because we're giving all that to Him. It's a wonderful place to be, and when it comes to our relationships, it gives back in dividends.

HOW TO RECEIVE AN APOLOGY

In addition to being able to take ownership of the offenses you cause, you also need to understand how to be on the receiving end of an apology. We often hear sermons on the importance of forgiving others, yet few of us have learned how to (a) hear an apology and (b) graciously respond to it.

For one thing, it's wise to respond to someone's apology the way you would want that person to hear and respond when you're the one apologizing.

Here are four ways you should not respond to an apology but probably have. We sure have.

The Preacher

It's amazing how the average parishioner can turn into Billy Graham in a matter of seconds when someone needs to be taught a lesson. The preacher response happens when an apology has been offered, but instead of just accepting the apology, the recipient starts to preach about what the offending person did wrong. Suddenly, this person is pulling scriptures from thin air, all showing how this grievance could have been avoided, before finally accepting the offered apology because "the Bible says to." Rather than forgiveness, the apologizer receives only shame in the guise of a spiritual response.

The Dismisser

This person acts like no offense was taken and, therefore, no apology is necessary. Oftentimes, the dismisser waves off an apology by

saying, "Don't give it another thought" or "It wasn't a big deal." And yet it was a big deal, and it did hurt. But because many of us don't like conflict, we simply dismiss the apology because we hate awkward moments or we don't want the apologizer to feel the pain we know all too well. But what the apologizer hears is that they wasted their time giving the apology. Or worse, that what they did really wasn't a big deal.

3 The Shamer

We feel three types of hurts:

1. **Embarrassment:** This is something we can genuinely laugh about later.

2. **Humiliation:** We've done something we feel bad about because we know we are better than what we did.

3. **Shame:** This is believing the bad thing someone says about us.

Shamers focus less on the apology and more on the offense. They try to convince the apologizer that he or she is defined by what they've done and will never be any different. The shamer does not accept the apology but instead makes the other person feel terrible by exploiting their feelings when they're at their most vulnerable. In that moment, the recipient of the apology holds power over the person offering it. If you've tried apologizing to a shamer, you know that no matter how hard you try or how many times you apologize, the shamer will make sure you know it can never be enough, and the shamer will be waiting and watching for your next offense.

4   The Collector

The collector remembers everything. When you apologize to a collector, you may as well sit down and get comfortable. The collector might accept your apology but, because he or she is worried for you, then proceeds to list every offense you've committed since you were eight. They throw out phrases like "Do you see the pattern here?" and "Is this ever going to change?" It seems loving, but the detailed history of wrongs makes the apologizer feel like change or improvement is out of reach, so why try?

5   And Then There's the Right Way

"I forgive you."

It's pretty simple. Maybe even offer a smile as you say it. Look into their eyes so they know you mean it. Give them a hug, and then, with genuine forgiveness, don't ever bring it up again or hold it against them in the friendship. It's onward and upward from here.

Here are a couple of other things to remember when apologizing.

First, do it in person if possible. No texting for sure.

Sit down, and make eye contact.

Finally, keep your expectations low. Few people give or receive apologies well. Try to focus on the person's effort, not their style, and do your best to be a role model in both areas.

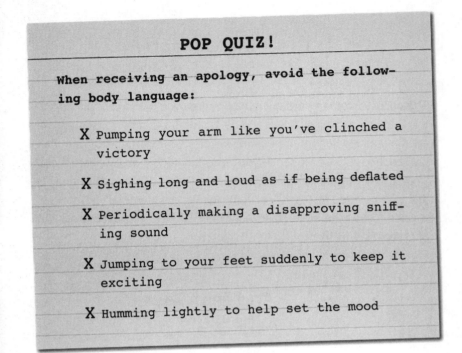

POP QUIZ!

When receiving an apology, avoid the following body language:

X Pumping your arm like you've clinched a victory

X Sighing long and loud as if being deflated

X Periodically making a disapproving sniffing sound

X Jumping to your feet suddenly to keep it exciting

X Humming lightly to help set the mood

KEEP A SHORT LIST

Go ahead and be angry. You do well to be angry—but don't use your anger as fuel for revenge. And don't stay angry. Don't go to bed angry. Don't give the Devil that kind of foothold in your life.

— EPHESIANS 4-26-27, *MSG*

Smart people know how to hold their tongue; their grandeur is to forgive and forget.

— PROVERBS 19-11, *MSG*

"Don't drive angry! Don't drive angry!"

— BILL MURRAY *in Groundhog Day*

The more you grow as a person and as a Christian, the fewer apologies you should need to receive in your life. You begin to realize a couple of things after a while, the first being that you're not as righteous as you think you are. This understanding makes it very hard to rise up in righteous indignation when you're still dealing with your own issues.

And the thing about being a Christian is, God's great at letting you know about your issues. The minute you think you've conquered one aspect of your life, He brings another to the surface. It seems sometimes there is an endless stream of false motives, unforgiveness, hang-ups, habits, and sins in our lives that are waiting to be dealt with.

And while we're dealing with these, we become hyperaware of God's amazing grace. We begin to recognize His merciful hand in our lives, and it is this recognition that allows us to begin to keep a short list of offenses and hurts.

A very short list.

By the way, calling people out on their shortcomings and sins, while popular in our culture, is not cool in our walk of faith. Every time you turn on your phone, tune in to the news, or open your laptop, you find an offense list all ready and waiting for your approval. Prompted by indignant email headlines, social media rants, or a friend not texting us back or using a questionable emoji, offense has become the norm for most of us.

So what kind of strange people not only let offense roll off their backs but also are quick to apologize when they themselves have offended someone?

Tommy: Sasquatch.

Eddie: Um, I believe we're talking about Christians. People of God. A peculiar people, as it were.

Tommy: Did you just go British?

Eddie: It's a quirk of mine.

Tommy: One of the many things that doesn't offend me about you. See what I did there?

Eddie: Buddy, I'm not sure you're totally catching on to this.

Tommy: Sure I am. The idea is that I have a ton of shortcomings.

Eddie: Okay, yes. Continue. I like where you're going with this.

Tommy: Tons of quirks. Some bad habits. And you know this about me.

Eddie: Correctamundo! You are totally nailing this.

Tommy: To be my friend, you're going to have to put up with a lot. At some point, to get along, you have to just say to some things, "It is what it is."

Eddie: It's practically our friendship motto. I mean, one of us may be doing more of the heavy lifting, but you're explaining it well.

Tommy: Thank you! Wait, what?

Eddie: The point being, friendships are about being willing to say "I'm sorry" when you're wrong, walk through the tunnel of chaos as needed, and hug it out on the other side.

Tommy: You might go into a friendship expecting it to be perfect, but sooner or later—usually sooner—you realize it won't be. But once you get past the disappointment, there's a kind of calm that comes over you as you learn to accept the friendship for what it is.

Eddie: Make sure the important aspects of friendship are there, of course, but then accept the friend for who they are.

Tommy: You celebrate the good and keep a short list of the bad. Focus on working on yourself, and it's amazing what that can do for a friendship. Or any relationship.

Eddie: Amen to that, my friend.

Tommy: Also, I am 100 percent aware that you just let me take most of the responsibility for being the one with all the shortcomings. And as an example of how we handle that, I would like us to discuss this now in front of God and everyone reading this book.

Eddie: Oh, buddy, that would be great. I'd love to do that.

Tommy: Excellent.

Eddie: HOWEVER, we have come to the end of this chapter.

Tommy: What?

Eddie: Yep. Man, I am as bummed as you are. I would really love to go through all my inadequacies with you, God, and our readers.

Tommy: But we're the ones deciding when to—

Eddie: So sad. Next chapter. Move on.

1. **Ask God to help you forgive those who've offended you.** Ask for His wisdom about whether a grievance should be addressed or let go.
2. **Make a list of things, small and big, you think people in your life have been kind to forgive you for.** Ask the Lord to help you recall these things when you're tempted to take offense at the actions or words of another.
3. **Ask the Lord to give you courage to apologize** to the people in your life, and ask Him to bring a good harvest from it.

CHAPTER 8
INTERRUPTI—

W hy does anyone work a garden or farm a tract of land? It's hard work. It soils the clothes. It can throw out your back, depending on the shape you're in. But all that work is done in the name of producing something—something good (food) or something lovely (flowers). Even the tiny seeds that are created may spread life through the future labors of others.

So throughout this book, we've talked about digging in the dirt of friendship. Tilling the ground, so to speak. And we've talked a bit about what those moments look like, whether it's a willingness to ride the giant goose/swan into the tunnel of chaos or learning to own up to mistakes. That's the digging. That's the dirt.

With that in mind, then, what does it all produce? Looking back on your relationships, what evidence of a harvest can you point to after years of putting in this kind of effort?

Examining the fruits of a friendship can help you decide many things about the relationship. What you're willing to give up and what has been given up for you are great indicators of the strength and longevity potential of your friendship.

Saying Yes

When we were young, we said yes to almost everything.

"Wanna play hide-and-seek?"

"Wanna catch the new *Star Wars* movie?"

"Wanna make some popcorn, pitch a tent in the backyard, and tell ghost stories all night?"

But for most of us, as we become adults, our default answer to any invitation begins to change from yes to no. How often do we turn down dinner out, a late-night party, or a Bible study at church in exchange for an evening on the couch at home?

Our culture demands a lot from us. Between working long hours, commuting a couple more, taking care of the family, doing household chores and repairs, and keeping up on the latest tweets, memes, and fainting goat videos, it can drain us, slowly shrinking our world to the point that we automatically say no to everything. And sometimes that's a good thing. After all, we clearly have to prioritize our time, and our priorities shift at every stage of life.

But in order to maintain long-term relationships, there must be exceptions to the rule of guarding your space and time. While you don't want to slide into people-pleasing, your attitude toward a friend should begin with a presumptive yes and go from there.

Of course, it's relatively easy to say yes to all the fun stuff, but what about things that ordinarily you don't have time for? Or that might cause you to think, I don't have the energy for that today. A friend needs an emergency babysitter or help getting a couch up two flights of stairs. How do you prioritize your time in a way that honors your friendships and makes positive impacts on the people in your various circles?

Tommy: Like that time at the barbecue restaurant!

Eddie: You have to be more specific. There's been a lot of barbecue.

Tommy: Cholesterol numbers don't lie. You were in town for work one day, and that night, my family and I were going to a barbecue restaurant for my dad's birthday.

Eddie: I remember, yeah.

Tommy: And I asked, "Do you want to come?"

Eddie: I said, "Sure, I'll come." I think I ordered pulled pork, chopped beef, ribs, and baked beans.

[*long pause*]

Eddie: Is that the story?

Tommy: It illustrates.

Eddie: I think it needs more.

Tommy: Well, the point is, you could've just gone back to your hotel or something. But instead, you said yes to something most people would have said no to, my dad's seventy-sixth birthday. No one says yes to their friend's dad's birthday!

Eddie: I said yes to spending time with you and your family. I love your family.

Tommy: That's it.

Eddie: I think we need a better story.

Tommy: I'm happy with it.

Eddie: I feel we can do better.

Tommy: That's one of the things that makes us great.

Eddie: What?

Tommy: Your discontentedness with my contentedness.

Looking at how Jesus used His time can help us understand how we might better choose to use ours. How Jesus used His time drove His disciples absolutely crazy. These twelve guys are depicted in the Gospels—half of which they wrote—as being utterly baffled by their Teacher's choices concerning when and where to be. They always had an agenda for Jesus, but He never stuck to it. He was so popular and so important, yet He made time for children and "the least of these." He seemed to have little patience with religious pomp and public piety but went out of His way—sometimes many miles out of the way—to connect with flawed and hurting people on a deeply personal level.

Let's take a closer look at three ways Jesus managed His time with people.

JESUS TOOK TIME FOR ONE-ON-ONE ENCOUNTERS

There's a fantastic story in the Gospel of John about a Pharisee named Nicodemus. Generally speaking, the Pharisees were not huge fans of Jesus. He disrupted a system they had securely in place and called into question everything they taught, from their views on God to their self-righteous attitudes and man-made rules. So surely it was surprising to those who witnessed the moment when Nicodemus showed up in the night to speak to Jesus.

Imagine, if you will, you've had a long day, and you finally get to sit down, get off your feet, and eat a nice hot bowl of chili when suddenly there's a knock at your door. Someone wants your time. Your attention. And you don't even know them that well.

You can hear it, can't you? The long, dreadful sigh escaping from your mouth as you push yourself off your comfortable couch and go see what they want.

But for Jesus, this was how He operated. He told us so, saying that if we knocked at the door, He would open it for us. And here Nicodemus was literally knocking at the door, so Jesus answered it.

Perhaps He took Nicodemus to a quiet place where they could have the discussion. John 3:1–21 describes the encounter. Nicodemus, cloaked in the darkness of the night (perhaps to avoid drawing the attention of his fellow Pharisees), asks heavy questions about salvation, and Jesus takes the time to answer them, even though He's been preaching and teaching these same ideas in the public forums.

Jesus wanted to plant a seed. He wanted Nicodemus to understand and was willing to spend one-on-one time with him to do that.

In our own lives, remembering that one-on-one encounters can grow relationships will help us be better friends and neighbors.

Jesus Welcomed Interruptions

The disciples. Oh, these poor guys. It's amusing to think about what they experienced as they followed Jesus around during His ministry. It's not that their intentions were bad. They were often just trying to move Jesus through crowds in order to get Him to important places and engagements. They knew He was preaching the truth, and they were eager to see the word spread. Logic told them that Jesus needed to be in this place, where He could make the most of His time and opportunities.

Imagine what it might have felt like, then, to watch Jesus get interrupted along the way. It must've been puzzling and a bit irksome to witness Him stopping to talk with a blind beggar or a tax collector perched in a tree. Can't you just see the disciples? Putting their hands over their faces, shaking their heads, trying desperately to understand why Jesus keeps allowing all these interruptions?

Take the story told in Mark 5. Jairus, a well-known leader in the community, comes to Jesus desperate and pleading for Him to come heal his daughter. She's dying, Jairus tells Him. Will He come?

Jesus agrees, and the disciples are pushing through the throng of people, rushing Him toward Jairus's home when suddenly Jesus stops. He turns and asks, "Who touched my robe?"

The disciples must have been befuddled at this point. They're in the middle of this crowd that keeps pressing in toward Jesus, and Jesus is asking who touched His robe. Perhaps one of them blurted out, "Um . . . everyone?"

We discover that a woman with a long-term illness has been healed by her faith, knowing if she could just touch His robe, she'd be healed. In the meantime, during this interruption, messengers arrive with the news that Jairus's daughter has passed away.

Surely, from the disciples' point of view, the situation looks hopeless. The little girl is dead. If Jesus hadn't gotten distracted, maybe He would have made it in time to heal her.

The story goes on to reveal one of Jesus' biggest miracles, as He brings the girl back to life. But the story also illustrates one of Jesus' many wonderful traits, which was that He was willing to be interrupted for the sake of connection, of relationship.

Jesus didn't mind people or the constant interruptions. We must drive Him crazy, yet He still interacts with us, still has time for us, still says yes to giving us His attention. Jesus knows the secret—that every interruption has the power to be an encounter of eternal significance. But it all begins with a yes.

In much the same way, keeping our agenda on a loose leash will allow relational interruptions into our lives. This approach allows us to prioritize people over agendas.

JESUS NOTICED PEOPLE

We have a lot to do, and in our society, we tend to interact with a lot of people. So it's tempting to see them as groups instead of as individuals. You rush in, have a meeting with ten other people, and are glad to escape with some dignity intact. It can be overwhelming sometimes.

But Jesus lived His life differently.

He had the most important job in the entire world, but when the disciples brushed off the children who wanted to climb onto His lap, Jesus rebuked them and called the children to come to Him.

When thousands of people needed to be fed, Jesus noticed a little boy with a small basket of fish and bread and called him over to help.

When traveling through a Samaritan village, He noticed a woman drawing water at the well, and sat down to speak with her about her life.

The disciples were just twelve ordinary men whom Jesus noticed and took the time to invest in.

You, too, have been the object of someone's attention—a parent, a spouse, a friend. It's a cherished moment when you're noticed.

Taking the time to notice those around us makes a real difference in their lives. The fast pace of our society leaves many feeling invisible. But Jesus made sure that those who felt left behind by society had His attention.

Who in your life, in your circles, could use your attention?

Eddie: I've got the story! I've got the perfect story.

Tommy: Okay, I don't know what could beat barbecue, but go ahead.

Eddie: Hospital food.

Tommy: Your palate has changed over the years, my friend.

Eddie: I'm telling that amazing story of when you came to see me in the hospital. Let me tell it.

Tommy: I wasn't even going to try to stop you.

Eddie: So I'm having surgery, and it's not a small surgery, so I'm a little nervous.

Tommy: Understandable.

Eddie: And so I'm about to go into surgery, and who shows up in my room?

Tommy: [*looks at him blankly*]

Eddie: YOU!

Tommy: I was hoping to take a couple of pics of you unconscious.

Eddie: You don't miss an opportunity to take pictures of me when I'm sleeping.

Tommy: I know! I'm going to publish a book someday with all the pictures I've taken over the years.

Eddie: Something is seriously wrong with you.

Tommy: It's going to be a coffee table book. Tons of pictures of you sleeping. Wanna know the title?

Eddie: No.

Tommy: *While You Were Sleeping: Moments I Remember but Eddie Never Will.*

Eddie: You are so weird. Why don't you just post stuff to social media like a normal person?

Tommy: Social media is of the devil.

Eddie: Anyway . . . you had driven three and half hours just to be with me and pray over me before I went into surgery. That meant so much. It really did. You knew I had many people surrounding me and helping me, but you still came. And then, at the end of the day, you drove back home that night. You did all that for me!

Tommy: You're wel—

Eddie: And you know who else came after you left? Our buddy David Rogers. And you know, David was there all evening! I mean, he was, like, dabbing my head with a cool washrag and the whole bit. Do you know he stayed all night? The guy had a packed day the next day, but I woke up at 5 a.m., and he was still there! He sent Steph home to get some sleep, and he stayed with me. Isn't that amazing?

Tommy: [*another blank stare*]

Eddie: What?

Tommy: I thought this was about how I was amazing.

Eddie: Oh . . . buddy . . . you're amazing. That was a huge deal what you did! You drove—

[*Tommy stomps away dramatically*]

Eddie: Buddy . . . oh . . . come back. I was just giving examp—. Buddy, wait, come back . . .

Whether stopping for a moment at the deli to ask how the owner's wife is doing or making a long drive to be with your friend in his worst hour, small yeses of time make a big difference, and big yeses make a huge difference. We need to recognize that God is not interested in our agenda for the day. With prayer and a willing heart, imagine what could happen if we began our mornings by asking God, "What do you want me to do today? Who do you want me to see?"

WORKING THROUGH HURTS, HANG-UPS, AND HABITS

The longer the friendship where trust has been built, where yeses have been given, where tunnels of chaos have been walked, the more natural the process of working together through hurts, hang-ups, and habits will become. This emerging aspect of a friendship might sound exhausting. After all, most of us want to stuff those parts of ourselves deep into our pockets so nobody sees them.

But the great thing about a close friendship is that there is built-in accountability, as well as an ability for our friends to clearly see our blind spots.

And we do have blind spots, don't we?

While it may be hard to accept criticism and suggestions from people outside our closest circles, this kind of input is more palatable when you hear it from a close friend because you know he or she has your best interests at heart. While "fixing" one another's blind spots shouldn't be the goal of any relationship, such insights are a by-product of working in the dirt that's there for you if you're willing to listen. You may even come to a place of such trust that you're asking the question before the blind spot is pointed out.

Eddie: This'll be fun. What are my blind spots?

Tommy: Uh . . . I don't know if this is a good idea. This doesn't seem fun.

Eddie: I'm fine. I'm genuinely asking: What are my blind spots?

Tommy: Eh . . . okay. Um, well, you're a little—

Eddie: —too ambitious for my own good?

Tommy: This is going to go sideways.

Eddie: I don't know the power of my own intelligence?

Tommy: Nailed it.

Eddie: Was that it?

Tommy: Totally.

Eddie: Do you want to play?

Tommy: Not at all.

Eddie: But this is the section of the book where we talk about it.

Tommy: Not openly. We're suggesting that it comes about organically in a friendship. It's not a game show.

Eddie: But that could be fun! [in his best game-show host voice] What dysfunction is behind Door Number 3?

Tommy: You see it, right?

Eddie: See what?

Tommy: Never mind. Let's tell the story of when we went shopping for camping supplies.

Eddie: Yes! We were doing this weeklong gig at a youth camp . . .

Tommy: So we're at Walmart, getting supplies for the week. And by "supplies," I mean water bottles, granola bars, and surround sound stereo systems. Plus, individual coffee makers because, apparently, we couldn't share a pot.

Eddie: And a state-of-the-art breakfast sandwich maker that cooked your egg, toasted your muffin, and heated the Canadian bacon all at the same time! I still have mine in the attic. Can't get rid of it.

Tommy: Me too!

Eddie: But at one point, we looked at our two full carts, and one of us said—

Tommy: "I think we have everything we need now."

Eddie: "I think we have everything we need now."

Tommy: Yeah, that was a huge habit we had to break.

Eddie: We still joke about it today, usually after one of us purchases something frivolous. "I think we have everything we need now."

Tommy: And that, my friend, is what we say in our friendship. "I think we have everything we need now."

Eddie: [tears shining in his eyes] Buuuuddddyyy . . .

Tommy: That was good, eh? Such a nice, poetic turn.

Eddie: Totally. Nobody even remembers our bad habit now.

This kind of accountability occurs more willingly than you might imagine. You begin to ask one another questions:

"Am I being a good parent if I do this?"

"Can you help me stay on my workout schedule?"

"I need to know, do you see me as [fill in the blank]?"

Trusting the source of the feedback makes all the difference in working through hurts, hang-ups, and habits.

As an inner-circle friendship unfolds, you'll find yourself revealing some deep hurts in your life. We all have them. But a good friend can help you find perspective and walk you through the healing, even if it's only by being a good listener.

Then there are those mental and emotional issues in our lives that may seem difficult to overcome. We call them hang-ups. Whether it's fear, anger, unforgiveness or something else, they can be hard to carry alone. A friend can help lighten the load, so don't be afraid to ask.

As for your habits (or addictions)—don't be afraid to share what you're struggling with or ask for help. Trust that a good friend will care enough to walk through it with you, whether assisting you with finding help, holding you accountable, or something else. Remember, being cared for cannot be cherished enough. Many want and need this kind of friend but don't have one, so don't take yours for granted.

There's a Swedish proverb that goes like this: Shared joy is a double joy. Shared sorrow is half a sorrow.

Eddie: That doesn't sound Swedish.

Tommy: Why not?

Eddie: If it were a Swedish proverb, it would say, "Delad glädje är en dubbel glädje. Delad sorg är halv sorg."

Tommy: What just happened?

Eddie: I translated it from American to Swedish.

Tommy: It's English, not American.

Eddie: I still spoke Swedish.

Tommy: You Google-translated it.

Eddie: I love Swedish fish.

Tommy: As long as you have interrupted the chapter, let's tell another story.

Eddie: Do you have one about a "delad sorg"?

Tommy: A shared sorrow? Yes, I do.

Eddie: Amazing!

Tommy: It's the spring of 2005, and we're headed to Houston to do a gig.

Eddie: I remember this. The night before we left, you'd been to visit your grandpa.

Tommy: Yep. My Pawpa was one of my life heroes. I remember spending the week with him and my Meme over summer breaks. Every afternoon, when I would lay down on the couch to take a nap, Pawpa would sit in the chair across the room, pick up his Bible, and read. I still have that Bible. It is worn out.

Eddie: So we land in Houston, and per usual, as the plane taxis to the terminal, we both turn on our cell phones and check for texts or voicemail messages.

Tommy: I did not have any.

Eddie: I had one. Just one.

Tommy: I noticed you listening very intently to the voicemail. I wasn't sure what was going on, but I knew it was serious.

Eddie: I finished listening, took a deep breath, and looked at you and said, "Buddy, I am so sorry, but your Pawpa just passed away."

Tommy: Yep.

Eddie: Your family didn't want to leave a voicemail for you about it, so they called me and asked me to share it with you.

Tommy: I'll never forget that moment. The world was a little less safe, a little scarier, and I was a whole lot hurt. But I knew that the guy sitting next to me with his hand on my shoulder would walk this path with me and help carry the load of sorrow that had just landed on me.

KEEPING PHYSICAL RELICS

The idea of keeping relics from a friendship might seem strange to some, but these small mementos can be great reminders during difficult times of the cherished treasure you have in your friend.

Through the years, we have had amazing experiences together. We've performed all over the country, taken vacations together, shared hilarious moments on airplanes and car rides.

We've written each other letters of thanks and expressions of emotion, kept movie tickets and receipts, held on to small trophies from seasons of victory, and more. Here are a few items you might find around our homes that remind us of our friendship.

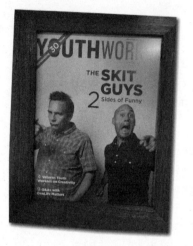

BONUS CONTENT!

Upcoming Coffee Table Book!

WHILE YOU WERE SLEEPING:
Moments I Remember but
Eddie Never Will

Think of a good friend. What are some relics, emotional or physical, that you have kept to remind you of that friendship? Take time to share these with your friend today.

CHAPTER 9

WHO'S (GOT) YOUR SIX?

"If you live to be a hundred, I want to live to be a hundred minus one day, so I never have to live without you."

— **WINNIE-THE-POOH** *to his friend Piglet*
Pooh's Little Instruction Book

This is a chapter on life. But we're going to start it by talking about death—

Tommy: Holy cow! Who is writing this book?

Eddie: What are you talking about?

Tommy: How do you start a chapter about life with a quote about death from Winnie-the-Pooh?!

Eddie: It seems like a pretty nice sentiment about life and friendship.

Tommy: But he's talking to Piglet! Why are we drawing everyone's attention to the impending death of two of the most loveable characters of all time?

Eddie: They are fictional characters. No one is actually dying here.

Tommy: That's just great! Now everyone who believes in Winnie-the-Pooh and Piglet knows they're not real! One second we're mourning their death, then BOOM, you hit us with the news that they're not real. Nice work, Mr. James.

Eddie: Oh bother.

BEGIN WITH THE END IN MIND

As we've talked through the principles of how to build a strong and lasting friendship, you may have noticed that we've subtly encouraged you to play the long game, to have the end in mind as you build your relationships.

Though it may seem a little morbid to think of friendship in this way, it's more about how you relate to others in life, not in death. But it's often in death where we see the impact people have had on each other, isn't it? From their funeral alone, you can tell who a person's closest friends were.

With that in mind, we want you to think about this for a moment: Who might carry your casket? Or who might speak at your funeral and share fond remembrances of your time together?

Perhaps you've had the experience of being a pallbearer. You grab the bar on the casket, along with five others, bearing together the physical and emotional weight of it. You carefully place the casket inside a hearse and then escort your friend to his or her final resting place. There's nothing quite like it.

The six who honor you by carrying your casket should be six people who at one time carried your mat. The people who stand and speak of you in the end should be those you trusted to know your brokenness and pain. In life, they were each willing to carry you as far as you needed to be carried. They couldn't fix you but were willing to take you to someone who could. These six left a wide-open space for you in their lives. And here they are, still by your side when life is over.

If there is someone in your life who you believe will one day carry your casket, make sure he or she is also a person who will get down on their knees and work in the dirt of life with you.

We're talking about people who know all your secrets and stick around anyway. They don't leave you at the rodeo. They ride the big goose with you into the tunnel of chaos. In military terms, these six have "got your six." And you've got theirs. Your life means something to them, and their lives mean something to you.

Some of your six may be people who don't do life with you on a day-to-day basis but were pivotal in certain chapters in your life. There is honor there for them. There is a forever friendship. There was enough life done together that they've earned their spot.

In the end, the people who will carry you in your death are the people who carried you in life. They are part of your trajectory. They are woven into your tapestry. You've worked hard to make sure they have stayed in your life.

CBS News ran a touching story of two buddies who carry on a strange tradition. Every week, rain or shine, Nashville neighbors Andy Gullahorn and Gabe Scott leave their homes at the exact same time. They both go for a walk through their neighborhood. And every time, at the same spot, they cross paths. When they do, they have a peculiar ritual: they clap, snap their fingers, and give each other a high five. Then they turn around and go home. Rather than just picking up the phone or sending a text, this is their way of saying hi.

They're both touring musicians, so they started this ritual as a way of keeping in touch. Andy even keeps a journal in which he records every high five.

But after 312 high fives, the encounters suddenly stopped.

Gabe was hospitalized with encephalitis, a severe swelling of the brain. He recovered, but it left him with crippling amnesia. He could barely remember anything from his life before.

Visiting him at the hospital, Andy had a strange request for his friend, who no longer recognized him. He said, "Gabe, this is going to sound really weird, but I need you to do something for me. Give me a high five."

And like riding a bike, Gabe said, "When the moment happened, my body just did what it's been doing for years—clap, snap, high five." He believes that not just the mechanics of the ritual but also the friendship part of it were so burned into his body memory, that's what came out.

Eddie: [*sniffling*] That story brings a tear to my eye.

Tommy: I know!

Eddie: Do we have a tradition like that?

Tommy: Two large pizzas, but we had to quit that. Hey, here's a great place to tell the whole story of how you came to Jesus.

Eddie: September of 1987.

Tommy: Yes. You were in a terrible place in life.

Eddie: That's true. I was a senior, this was my last play, and I didn't get cast.

Tommy: For readers who are sports fans, that's like getting cut from the team.

Eddie: Exactly.

Tommy: But with less hand-eye coordination.

Eddie: Less popularity.

Tommy: Less athlete's foot fungus.

Eddie: That's too far.

Tommy: Sorry. I was just itching to add to the discussion.

Eddie: And it should be noted I killed the audition. I was totally baffled as to why I didn't get cast.

Tommy: On the other hand, I was—

Eddie: Walking on water, basically. You'd been bribed to go on a mission trip where the Holy Spirit sparked a forest fire in your heart, and you came back all Jesus-y.

Tommy: Sooo Jesus-y. And it should be mentioned that I was now a freshman in college, and you were a senior in high school, and that's kind of two different worlds.

Eddie: I figured it was a phase you'd grow out of.

Tommy: So we were still friends but in totally different places.

Eddie: You'd asked me to do a couple of skits with you at church. I did them, but I thought they were really cheesy. I mean, I was ready to head to New York to help out Mike Myers and Dana Carvey on *SNL*. Not to say I could have made it, but that was the dream.

Tommy: Then one day, I called you at your job, working produce at Food World, with the most awkward church invite ever. I'd never invited anyone to church before in my life. All I knew is that you needed Jesus. So you come to the phone, and I'm all like, "Hey, tomorrow night we're having this deal at church. It's like a revival thing."

Eddie: "Uh-huh."

Tommy: "And I wanted to know if you wanted to come."

Eddie: [silence]

Tommy: "There's going to be pizza."

Eddie: "Okay, sure. Yeah. I got nothing better to do."

Tommy: And there's a beautiful lesson here because that's all I did. God did the rest. All I knew was that my friend needed Jesus. At the end of the service that night, there's this altar call, and they ask if anyone wants to accept Christ as their Lord and Savior. I'm praying and praying and praying for you. Then I open my eyes and glance over at you—and you're gone.

Eddie: I went to the front, a pastor prayed with me, and I accepted Jesus. What a gift you gave me. What a tremendous mat you carried for me!

Can you look back on your own life and see the hand of God at work? Can you identify a moment in your life when you didn't get cast in the play, when things didn't work out like you wanted, but that opened a God gap—a space He arranged to put you in so He could do a good work in you? At some point, we all have a plan for where we think we want to go, what we want to do with our lives. And maybe we'd be really good at that thing. But God often has His own plans for us, and if we follow His lead, incredible things can happen.

Side note: He loves to use other people to take you there.

WATCHING FOR THE GOD MOMENTS

When two Christians become friends, there's another amazing dynamic at work in the relationship—a spiritual dynamic. We pray for our friends. We edify them by sharing the Word of God. If we need to admonish them, we have biblical principles to fall back on. A threefold cord is not quickly broken (Ecclesiastes 4:12), and the connection between two good friends is dramatically stronger when the third cord is Jesus Christ.

Some of the best times in a relationship are when two friends get to watch each other experience transcendent moments. But when God is involved, going through seasons of difficulty together can be just as amazing. The fact is, we never stop changing and growing, even when we don't want to. And the older we get, hopefully, the less our lives are filled with chaos. But there are still seasons when we may find our world turned upside down. In those moments, we can't do it alone.

Death is a season. It's the final season on earth. However, if you will allow God to work in you and through you to cultivate meaningful relationships, your last season can be filled with the people you will need and want there.

If you know who your six are, make sure they know it, too. Make it part of your friendship vernacular: "You know you're part of my six. If I die before you, I want you to be right there alongside me, carrying me to my final resting place." Even in the somberness of that statement, there is beauty. Those carrying your casket are the people who carried you through life. They were the ones who held you up when the rest of life let you down. They were the calm in the midst of your storms.

Tommy: Hi, my name is Tommy, and I am a faithful believer in Jesus Christ who has struggled with alcohol.

Eddie: Hey . . . you don't have to do this.

Tommy: No, I want to. It might just help someone, and it speaks to what we're talking about.

Eddie: Okay, I'll be right here with you.

Tommy: I spent thirtysomething years of my life never touching a drop of alcohol. Then when I did, my addictive personality took over, and I spent the next ten years craving the stuff. While my lifestyle didn't afford me the opportunity to drink often, when I did, I drank as much as I could. One night, after spending some time in an airport lounge, I flew home from an event, hopped in my car, and drove home drunk. I made it safely home by God's grace alone. The next morning, when I woke up, the Lord brought to mind Psalm 143:8 (NIV): "Let the morning bring me word of your unfailing love." I was heartbroken and ashamed of my actions and very aware that something had to change. I walked into where my wife was sitting and apologized for not being honest with her. I promised her I was going to change. I then immediately picked up the phone and called Eddie. I told him I was an alcoholic and that if I was going to make it, I would need his support and accountability. My story is much longer, and there is much more to my recovery, but the point is, I knew who I could count on. I knew who would help me carry this burden. I knew who I could trust—my best friend, Eddie James. By God's grace, and with the help of Celebrate Recovery, I am able to say I have not taken a drink since that fateful night.

Eddie: Good job.

Tommy: Thanks. And thanks for always being there.

Eddie: Always will be.

SIX WAYS TO KEEP YOUR SIX

The hope, of course, is that we all get to live long lives. But whether our lives are short or long, there are some things we can do in the time we have on earth to better ensure the longevity of our relationships.

The truth is, the older we get, the harder friendships are to maintain. Gone are the days of freewheeling and shirking responsibility.

Now we have families, jobs, bills to pay, and aging parents to care for. Friendships that were once easy now take intentional effort, not because the friendships are hard but because there's a lot going on in your life. Your attention is being pulled in a hundred directions, so the decision to wait and call your friend tomorrow can quickly stretch to days or weeks, and the next thing you know, it's been a year since you've talked.

But if you're serious about playing the long game, about cultivating and maintaining a handful of close friendships, we have a list of things you can do to ensure that time, distance, and responsibilities won't leave you with nobody to carry your casket. Now, some of these suggestions may come easily to you, while others may make you perspire like a celebrity contestant eating spicy chicken wings on camera because "that's just not me." However, making these investments—some bigger, some smaller—will go a long way toward cementing a lifelong friendship.

1   Learn Their Language

We left out a tiny little word in this headline because we didn't want to freak you out. We want to kind of ease you into this because unless you're a Gary Chapman fan, this is going to sound weird. If you have no idea who Gary Chapman is, stay with us as we explain. It'll be worth it.

Years ago, Dr. Chapman, an author and counselor, wrote a book called *The Five Love Languages*, which outlines five basic ways men and women like to receive affection. If you know a person's love language, you can more effectively express your affection for that individual. This clearly works within marriages, but it turns out it also works with children, friends, and even coworkers. Here are the five languages:

- Words of Affirmation

- Quality Time

- Physical Touch

- Acts of Service

- Receiving Gifts

You can take a quiz to find out what yours is, and once you know it, you'll understand yourself a little better. And once you learn the love languages others speak, you'll be able to identify how best to communicate with them.

For example, a "quality time" friend might really appreciate going to get coffee with you, whereas a "physical touch" person might need those hugs you're not used to offering. A "words of affirmation" friend is one who will most appreciate your texts. It's surprisingly simple once you know what is significant to them, and if you just pay attention, you'll soon figure out their language.

FIVE PHRASES TO AVOID WHEN DETERMINING A FRIEND'S LOVE LANGUAGE

X "When I touch your arm, how does that make your emotions feel?"

X "I broke into one of your Amazon lists. Boy, are you getting a surprise!"

X "You are amazing! Is that enough, or would you rather have coffee?"

X "I'm coming over to wash your dishes. No need to thank me! I'm kidding—I deeply and sincerely need you to."

X "On a scale of one to ten, how much do you want me to shovel your driveway?"

Write Letters

Texts are good. Phone calls are fantastic. But nothing beats a letter. Most everyone who receives a heartfelt letter keeps it. Not everyone is able to communicate their feelings face to face. But sitting down and writing a letter to someone you care about produces a harvest that can last a lifetime. You're able to say all you need to say, and your friend has a keepsake to which they can always refer back.

Letters are sometimes the very thing that can get you through the tunnel of chaos. In fact, letters are sometimes a great way to celebrate having walked through that tunnel. Letters don't need to be fancy or poetic; they just need to be from the heart. And if writing letters sounds so 1947, look for an opportunity to buy your friend a greeting card, even a funny one, but don't skip putting in the sentiment of how you appreciate and love this friendship.

E -

I saw this and thought of us. Who gets to have more fun than us at our jobs? I am continually amazed at what we get to do. I am continually thankful for such a friend as you. I pray that God will protect our ministry and take it places we can not even imagin. Most of all, I pray that He protects our friendship, because I believe we have something that most people will spend a lifetime looking for... true brotherhood & love.

I love you -

3 Keep Mementos

Mementos are a great physical reminder of the history of a relationship. A box full of game-day ticket stubs, birthday cards, maps from a road trip, and so on can be a wonderful reminder of the value of a particular relationship. In and of themselves, they don't really mean anything, but it is what they represent that carries the value.

4 Send Gifts

Gifts don't need to be expensive or frequent, but small gifts that have meaning attached are some of the best ways to celebrate a friendship. And sometimes, the funnier they are, the better. Whether it's a hilarious gag gift or something sentimental, the joy of receiving an unexpected package in the mail will put a smile on anyone's face.

Did your friend comment on how much she liked your bracelet? Take the time to send her one. Did your buddy remark on his aversion to glitter? Why not have some fun and hand him a specially wrapped glitter bomb? Such gifts create lasting memories that can go the distance through thick and thin.

5 Share Experiences

Time, distance, budget, and responsibility do a good job of getting in the way of life experiences, but it's well worth the effort to make them happen anyway. Whether it's a once-in-a-lifetime road trip to see Fenway Park, a skydiving adventure, or a yearly canoe trip, experiences can create lasting memories that you'll recount over and over when you're able to see each other again. Experiences can't be taken away. They don't burn down. They can't be stolen. They really are an ever-lasting gift.

Tell Them They Are One of Your Six

Talking with one another about the endgame lets a person know you fully expect them to be in your life your whole life, however long that is. Whether you ask them to be a pallbearer, to speak at your funeral, or to serve your favorite cookie at the funeral dinner, it's meaningful to another person to hear that you want them there for all of it.

POETS' CORNER

We've written a poem you're welcome to borrow in pursuit of your six. It's still a little rough, but you'll get the idea. We recommend putting it in a card or reading it at Applebee's over dinner.

I'm going to die

Maybe while eating pie.

I'll let out a sigh

But that's a good way to go.

Whatever the case

Eventually I'll be underground.

As terrible as that sounds

That's the way it is.

So I wanted to ask

If you'll carry my cask—

—et to my final resting place.

(pause)

I need to know by Tuesday.

Thanks.

Get a piece of paper and a pen. Write the date. Then write "My Six." Take some time to think of the names of the people who might be your six pallbearers or who you might invite to speak at your funeral. Next to each name, write out the reasons why. Whether they are family or friends, make intentional efforts to keep these six in your life. Cultivate these Garden friends. Put in the effort starting today.

Solid Gold 97.7 FM

700 South Kelly • Edmond, Oklahoma 73034 • (405) 348-9898

Dear Ed,

Thought I'd drop you a line befor I left for big Tenn.
I guess whenever I go on a trip it reminds me that we don't
know what tommorow holds for us. It might sound corny, but
I want to set things straight befor I leave just to be prepared for the worst. The most important part of this letter
is to let you know that you are the best friend I have ever
had. Thanks for everything. When I called you today I wasn't
going to the audition unless you would go with me. When the
guy asked if I had confidence today, the only reason I could
say yes was because you were with me. You are my security.
I don't know what my life would have been without you and
I'm glad I don't know! Anyway, I hope you get the main idea
wich is this; YOU'RE THE BEST!!!!!!!!!!!!

On to bigger and better things, I called HLN (that's
in code incase any communist scum pigs get a hold of this
important document. I told her I would like to go out and
she said that would be great. I'm not sure if she likes me
or if it's friends or if she feels sorry or if it's our
families are so close or if I can make up some more ex-
cuses. So be proud of me for finding some courage.

This is the closing of my letter. Have a great week
and I'll give you a ring as soon as I get home.

                    Love Ja Buddy
                    Tommy

P.S.

I am so happy that the Lord is starting to work in your
life. When you get back from camp, let's start to help each
other live the kind of lives we should be living. I don't
know if you got that quiet time material or not. if you did
not I will leave it in my mailbox. Be sure you use it I
know you'll love it!!

FUNNY YOU SHOULD ASK

I n our ministry and in our lives, we believe in laughter. We believe in its power. We've seen laughter change people's lives. We've heard countless stories from people who've come to our shows for a few laughs and left totally changed from the inside out.

They laughed, and God entered.

He is, after all, the source of all true joy. And even as we perform silly skits and tell funny jokes, we do it in the name of the Lord for the purpose of bringing His Good News to as many people as possible.

But all good shows must end, friend, and this one is almost over.

So may we leave you with some final thoughts?

Laughter Breaks Down Walls . . .

Laughter is powerful. And it can be used for good or for evil.

For centuries, comedians and theologians alike have used humor to make a serious subject more palatable. Laughter can make even taboo subjects easier to talk about.

Indeed laughter has changed the moral ground of entire cultures. Think how often TV sitcoms have done that very thing in our own culture.

Ponder for a moment the effect laughter has had in your own life and in your relationships. Who makes you laugh? It seems like a simple question, but it can also be a question that guides you. A friend who can cause you to laugh at life—at circumstances, at problems, even at yourself—should be, if all other aspects of the friendship are healthy, a friend to keep.

At The Skit Guys, we take our ministry seriously but not ourselves. We love making God famous and having fun while we do it. Zoom conference calls with our staff, who live all over the country, can sometimes dissolve from agendas to hilarity. To work with us, you must love to laugh.

We believe God loves to laugh with us. Of course, much of what we do—our videos, our live shows, our movies—is about sharing His truth through the vehicle of humor. Sometimes in our live shows, even as we're making the audience laugh, we end up laughing ourselves. We don't try to stop it. Why would we?

In our own friendship, we keep life's hardships balanced with life's funny moments. If there's a moment to laugh, we'll take it. We never let it pass us by. Life is hard, so why would we not appreciate every opportunity we have to laugh? The funny can even be found in life's most difficult moments when looked at in the rearview mirror.

Have you ever seen a baby chuckle before he or she has learned self-consciousness? It's pure delight. Nobody teaches babies to laugh; they're born that way. Indeed, science tells us humans were made to laugh. Laughter releases endorphins, serotonin, and other feel-good hormones into our systems. Laughter acts as a salve, relieving stress, easing physical pain, and even helping us to heal faster.

God has a sense of humor, too. This shouldn't surprise us, because we are made in His image. He tells us in His Word there is a time to weep and a time to laugh (Ecclesiastes 3:4). We can see evidence of God's sense of humor in His creation. A giraffe alone can give us a good idea of how funny God is.

And the longer you know God, the more you'll discover that He loves to laugh with you. Yes, He will guide you through the difficult times in the hard journey of life. But as you seek Him, you will notice here and there that some of His answers are both wise and funny. For instance, He has a great little piece of advice about examining the log in your own eye before pointing out the speck of sawdust in your friend's. Keep an eye out for God's sense of humor, because it can spark real joy in us.

Remember this: God gets you. And He gets your sense of humor even if no one else does!

Now it's time . . .

. . . for Truth to Enter

As you ponder what you've read and consider the principles we've presented, here are some gentle reminders on how to allow truth to enter your life:

1. **To find the right people, you have to be the right kind of person.** If you are running a deficit in the assets that make a great friend, we urge you to take a hard look at your hurts, hang-ups, and habits. The effort to tackle these in your life can pay huge dividends. The work will be tough, but it will bring freedom, lead to great friendships, and heal the relationships already in your life.

2. **Honor your friends.** They may be in your life today or were in a season past. When you talk to, see, or think of one of these friends, remember to honor that person and show them love. Home in on what is really special between the two of you. The more you practice this, the stronger your bonds will be.

3. **Who are you holding in a mental prison?** You're playing Batman and reliving the pain, grabbing onto this person over and over and

yelling "YOU did this to me!" in your best Christian Bale growl. It's time to let them go. You may never get the "I'm sorry" moment you want, but you don't need it. Holding onto the hurt is only hurting your heart.

4. **Practice this book.** What does that mean? Read chapters, highlight sections, maybe journal your thoughts before moving on. Live out what you've learned here in the real world. Become your own Daniel LaRusso, and we will be your Mr. Miyagi, waiting to cry "Banzai!" when we meet.

5. **And through all the truth, *don't forget to laugh.***

Tommy: Hey, Ed, I really enjoyed our time going back to California recently, even though it was under sad circumstances.

Eddie: Yeah, saying goodbye to John Baker . . . that was a tough funeral. It makes me think about my six and the legacy I'll leave behind. I'm so thankful for what John Baker did for me and for millions of others through Celebrate Recovery. He was a dad to me. He helped me to grow from a boy to a man. He always had my back and always showed me love.

Tommy: I was honored to be by your side as you mourned and grieved.

Eddie: You know what I'll remember about that weekend as well, T? I will remember how much we laughed. Man, in forty-eight hours, you and I laughed a ton. Like, gut-busting, can't-breathe, stop-it-already-type laughter. Even in mourning, we found ourselves laughing like two best buddies from high school, laughing on this amazing playground we call Earth that God has given us all. Great laughter really does cause walls to tumble down and allows friends to be vulnerable.

Tommy: It's good to laugh. It's good medicine.

Eddie: Unless you break your leg. Then you just really need a doctor.

Tommy: That depends . . .

Eddie: On what?

Tommy: How well can you tell a joke.

A CKNOWLEDGMENTS

T his book came about because of a relationship that started in a Cracker Barrel when two sets of friends got together and talked about movies and friendship. Bill Reeves entered our lives a number of years ago and has helped us achieve a few dreams over the years, one being this book. Bill, thanks for catching the vision for what we have to offer alongside your Uncle Herschel's breakfast. And Brian Mitchell and Dave Schroeder, you both encouraged us to be ourselves as we put this book together. We hope people like us. Hopefully, they really, really like us!

Without the amazing Rene Gutteridge's writing, tweaking, and fleshing out, this book could not have been written. She makes us better daily. And this couldn't have been navigated with two voices speaking (literally) as a book without the sheer genius of Jay Howver. We'd also like to thank David Webb, Matt West, and the Dexterity team for the terrific insight and effort they poured into the project.

This friendship wouldn't be what it is without our wives, Angie Woodard and Stephanie James, who said yes long ago to this dynamic duo, and our kids, who have fostered the friendship as if we were family. I guess we sort of are!

And warm thanks to Wayne Slay, who made us business cards in the 80's and told his minister buddies about us, and Bob Johns, who flew us to Waco, Texas for our first gig in 1988.

And finally, special thanks to our Skit Guys family—Brian, Jina, Jen, Chris, Roni, Sarah, David, Carrie, Tylor, and Jonathan—a special group of people we love, who work behind the scenes, honoring God daily with their gifts and talents.

We'd also like to thank—

Tommy: I think we're out of time.

Eddie: What do you mean?

Tommy: They're playing the music. That's our cue to stop talking.

Eddie: This isn't an awards show.

Tommy: You don't know that. There might be an award someday. Hurry, off we go. We don't want them to get out that hook or kill the lights on us. That's so embarrassing.

Eddie: I think we passed embarrassment back in chapter 2, but I guess we gotta end somewhere.

Tommy: [*smiling and waving*] Come on. Smile. Wave. People are staring.

Eddie: Oh, boy. Fine. I'm smiling and waving . . . waving and smiling . . .

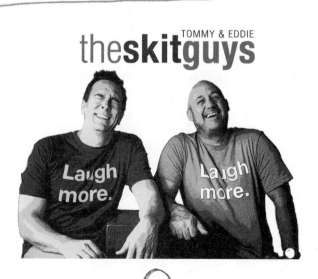

About the Authors

Tommy Woodard's illustrious career began around 1975 on the front porch of his home where his older (and bossier) sister, Debbie, would direct him in homemade plays. They would invite their parents, neighbors, and strangers walking by to sit on the lawn and enjoy their masterful works of art. He went on to perform in high school plays, where his favorite thing was to pretend to be different characters with his best buddy Eddie. (Who knew 30 years later they would be doing that and reaching millions through stage and screen?)

On top of being one half of The Skit Guys, Tommy has co-authored over a dozen publications with Eddie James, including *Skits That Teach* v.1 and 2, *Instant Skits*, *TV Shows That Teach*, and *Skit Training 101*. He also serves as a pastor at Newchurch in Oklahoma City. Tommy lives in Edmond, Oklahoma with his wife and kids.

For over thirty years, **Eddie James** has performed comedy sketches and improv on thousands of stages all over the world, acted in hundreds of short films and skits viewed by countless millions, and yet he is still brought to tears almost every day when he gets letters and emails from fans far and wide describing the personal impact The Skit Guys' sketches and short films have had on others' lives.

On top of being one half of The Skit Guys, Eddie has co-authored Videos That Teach books with Doug Fields, and he's also co-authored over a dozen publications with Tommy Woodard, including *Skits That Teach* v.1 and 2, *Instant Skits*, *TV Shows That Teach*, and *Skit Training 101*. Eddie lives with his wife and two daughters in Sachse, Texas, and is a creative consultant and online pastor at his church.

Rene Gutteridge has been writing professionally for twenty years, with published and produced work in fiction, comedy sketches, novelizations, non-fiction and screenwriting, and is co-director of WriterCon in Oklahoma City. Her novel *My Life as a Doormat* was adapted into the Hallmark movie *Love's Complicated*. She is head writer at Skit Guys Studios. When she's not writing, she's writing, or writing about writing or teaching writing. She lives with her family in Oklahoma City.

THE SKIT GUYS PODCAST

LISTEN AT

 access**more**.

OR WHEREVER YOU FIND PODCASTS

www.skitguys.com/sgtv

HERE ARE MORE GREAT WAYS TO BE ENCOURAGED EVERYWHERE YOU GO!

POSITIVE, ENCOURAGING

K-LOVE

Listen online at **KLOVE.com**

Download the app

Air1 worship now

Listen online at **Air1.com**

Download the app

accessmore.
FAITH-BASED PODCASTS

Listen online at **AccessMore.com**

Download the app

Learn more about at our books at
KLOVE.COM/BOOKS and **AIR1.COM/BOOKS**